D1751434

Don't Let Fear Have All The Fun

And Other Advice For Making
Bold Moves Even If You're Afraid

Monique Malcolm

Copyright © 2022 by Monique Malcolm

All rights reserved. No part of this publication may be reproduced, distributed, or transmitted in any form or by any means, including photocopying, recording, or other electronic or mechanical methods, without the prior written permission of the author/publisher, except in the case of brief quotations embodied in critical reviews and certain other noncommercial uses permitted by copyright law.

For permission requests, write to the author at: moniquemalcolm.com

Don't Let Fear Have All The Fun / Monique Malcolm—1st ed.

Paperback (Pink): 978-1-956989-08-3
Hardcover: 978-1-956989-09-0
Paperback (Yellow): 978-1-956989-10-6

Contents

Introduction 1

ADVICE #1
A Life Built On Fear Already Has Built-In Limitations. 11
ADVICE #2
Make Sure You Understand The True Cost
Of Listening To Fear 29
ADVICE #3
Name Your Fears And Take Back Your Power 47
ADVICE #4
Give More Energy To The Best-Case Scenario 65
ADVICE #5
Take Tiny Action To Build Your Courage 83
ADVICE #6
Celebrate Your Entire Journey 105
ADVICE #7
Find And Build Your Cheer Squad. 131
ADVICE #8
Treat Failure As An Event, Not An Endpoint 157

Conclusion 177
Resources 183
Acknowledgements 185
Author Bio 187

Praise for *Don't Let Fear Have All The Fun*

"I really enjoyed this new and approachable way of getting comfortable with fear. Monique's easy story-telling style instantly resonated and helped me see where fear is preventing me from making important decisions — and what to do about that."

GABRIELLE BLAIR

"This book is a must for anyone wanting to overcome their fears! Monique helps you push past your fear so you can accomplish your dreams and goals! Be prepared to become your best self and live your best life."

MELISSA ALLEN

"As humans, we often look at other people's situations and say what we would have done differently. Monique's transparent storytelling baits you into doing just that. She allows you to see how fear manipulated her life and compare it to your own. I hadn't realized just how much fear had stolen from me. It has stolen my time, my energy, my confidence, my reputation, my money, and certainly my joy."

ALGIE HENDRIETH

Dedication

Dedicated to Maurice Malcolm Junior and Joy Elaine Malcolm.

My cosmic connections. I see you amongst the stars,
and I love you forever.

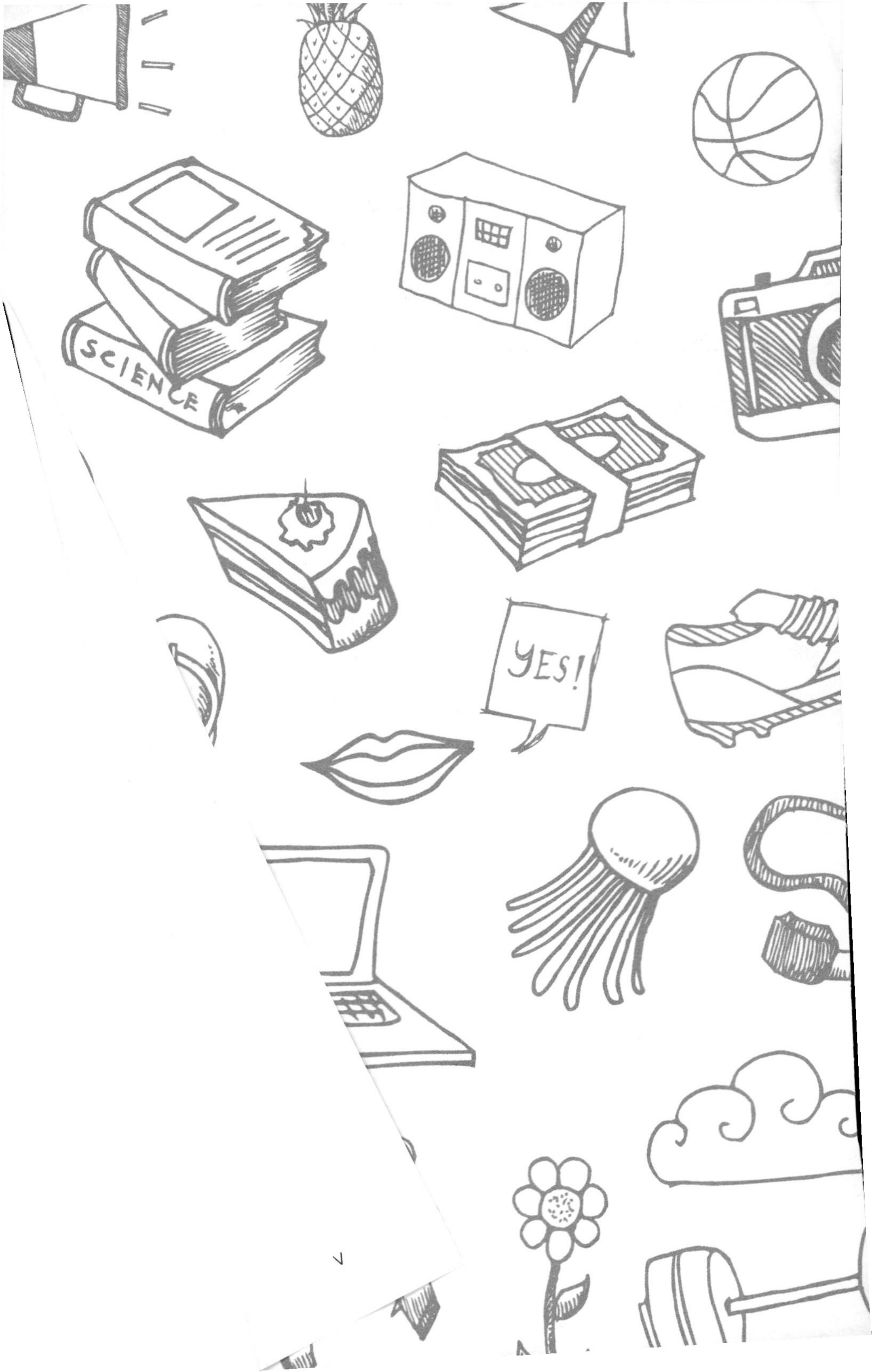
SCIENCE
YES!

INTRODUCTION

Don't Let Fear Have All The Fun

I was an honor student. I maintained a 4.0 GPA. I graduated ninth in my graduating class in high school.

And I only applied to my safety net college.

That doesn't seem right, does it?

Well, this is a book about fear, and as you'll soon realize, fear doesn't always follow logic. Before I get ahead of myself, let me share a story with you.

For as long as I can remember, my dad encouraged me to attend college. I never questioned whether or not I would attend. I always knew I would. When we talked about my future, his advice was always the same: "Go to school and make good grades so that you can go to college." That's precisely what I did.

I'm unsure if my dad realized how seriously I took his advice. I didn't just make good grades. I got excellent grades.

Here's a rundown of how I positioned myself as a prime academic candidate in high school:

* I enrolled in a magnet program focused on international studies, which required a more rigorous course curriculum than the standard graduation requirements. I knew it would look good and give my future college applications a competitive edge.

* As a freshman in high school, I registered for a seventh-period class after school to get ahead on my credits.
* My sophomore year, I took Spanish and Japanese to meet my foreign language credit requirements.
* I took classes every summer so I'd have more advanced course options during the regular school year.
* Throughout my coursework, I maintained a weighted 4.0-grade point average.
* By the beginning of my senior year, I had 23 of the 24 credits required for graduation. I opted for dual enrollment, allowing me to attend the local community college full-time as a senior.
* I graduated in the top 10 of my graduating class with 25 college credits.

I put in the work.

One evening during the fall of my senior year of high school, I proudly strutted into the kitchen with a brochure to announce my top choice for college. My dad had just come home from work and was standing in the doorway taking off his boots.

"I want to go to the University of Miami," I told him right before handing him the pamphlet.

In a resigned voice, he looked at me and said, "I can't afford that." It crushed me.

My dad's admission that he couldn't afford to send me to the University of Miami wasn't a shock. I always knew my path to college relied on scholarships and financial aid. It's the reason why I worked so hard academically. It had always been my plan to leverage my academic abilities as a way to pay for college.

Here is where things get illogical. Pay attention.

My dad feared that he couldn't afford to send me to college. I solved that problem by working hard to make myself a strong academic candidate. When it was time to play my cards and show the University of Miami the hand I had so expertly assembled, I chose to fold instead of playing.

More than twenty years later, I still think about that experience. The risk was minimal. All I had to lose was the time it took to prepare the application and a $75 application fee. What would have happened if I had played my hand?

I've narrowed my odds down to three things:

* I applied, got accepted, and was offered an excellent financial aid package.
* I applied but didn't get accepted.
* I applied and got accepted but wasn't offered enough financial aid.

In hindsight, none of those outcomes seem that bad. At the time, I viewed the situation through the lens of my father's fear. I was afraid I would burden my family financially if I got accepted to the University of Miami. Never mind that I worked hard to minimize the chance of that happening. I couldn't see past that fear, so I chose the safe option, a cheaper college closer to home.

I don't have many regrets in life, but not applying to the University of Miami is definitely in the top five. I didn't play my hand.

I only played myself.

I shared that story to illustrate a point—I know what it's like to live your life ruled by fear. I know how stifling it feels to have huge ambitions, work very hard, and still let fear overrule your plans.

My experience isn't unique. I'm willing to bet that $75 application fee that you have your own version of an "I didn't apply to my dream college" story. The ugly truth is that you have let fear run your life. I know this because I used to do it too. I did it for years. And now I can spot when it's happening a mile away. Here are some tell-tale signs:

Fear has made you afraid to pursue your creative ideas. It has fooled you into believing no one will find value in them. Convincing you that the ideas you want to bring to life aren't necessary. Whispering in your mind, "I'll fail, so why bother trying?"

Fear has caused you to overthink and second guess every little decision. It has forced you to stop and start over constantly. Making you seek validation for every decision. Now you find yourself frustrated, wheels spinning, and going nowhere.

Fear has caused you to settle in love or your career. You've heard the internal voice whispering, "You don't deserve this," for so long that you believe it. You accept any relationship or job handed to you because you are lucky to at least have something. You feel guilty that you dare to want more than the bare minimum for your life.

Fear has wrought havoc on your confidence. Keeping you small. Keeping you comfortable. Keeping you focused on doing the "safe" option. Fear always has the final say. You're reluctant to admit that you put fear in control and your life lacks luster.

The result of letting fear have the starring role in your life is that you're carrying around a garbage bag full of unmet desires, forgotten dreams, and unaccomplished goals, which impact your self-esteem, sense of purpose, and overall happiness.

    I can confidently say that fear is dictating your life's rules and having all the fun at your expense.

What It Means Not To Let Fear Have All The Fun

The first time I said, "Don't let fear have all the fun," it felt like fate. I was speaking to a group of women at a creative camp about the importance of learning to quiet your fear and go after your dreams. As I wrapped up my talk, I looked into the faces of the women hanging onto every word, some with tears in their eyes, and I felt a strong urge to leave them with a sense of hope, words that they could repeat to themselves anytime the fear inevitably showed up in their lives. I blurted out the first words that came to my mind. I knew as soon as the words left my mouth that I had said something powerful. I quickly scribbled the words down into the margins of my notes so I wouldn't forget them.

When I say, "Don't let fear have all the fun," what I mean is...

You have goals and ideas. Places you want to visit. Things you want to create. A purpose you wish to fulfill and a beautiful life to live. Don't let your fear make you so afraid of moving forward that you miss experiencing all the fun those things can bring.

The fun lies in setting goals and hitting them, or not hitting them but learning so much along the way. The fun is stretching and continuing to grow. The fun is doing exciting things with your life. The fun is knowing you tried instead of wondering what might have been. The fun comes from being afraid but doing it anyw

You don't have to be "fearless" to go after the things want in your life. You can be afraid, learn to quiet the boor voice of fear, and take the next small step anyway.

That's where the fun is.

What You'll Learn From This Book

In this book, I share the lessons I have learned about getting comfortable with fear and tell them through short stories. I am not making false promises or exaggerated claims. This is my lived experience, and these are the tips, steps, and strategies I have used to navigate my fears.

You will learn:

* Why being fearless is not the goal
* What the Chorus of Fear is and how it operates through the Levels of Apprehension
* How comfort and fear are allies
* The importance of acknowledging your fear to take back your power
  How to build courage in small doses
  Why you need to give more energy to the best-case scenario
  ow to get started and find your step one
  ctly how to build a support system for yourself that
  ed with people who are happy to cheer you on
  he most important thing you can do if you're
  f failure (most people get this wrong).

e, you won't learn any hacks or quick fixes for
That's not what this book is about. So I want
lear upfront.
s a fun, approachable, and impactful guide
now tackling fear is a heavy topic, but I
l as light-hearted and funny as it is pro-
ction despite being afraid is essential

I developed a unique way to describe fear (which you will learn in Chapter 1) filled with colorful metaphors. I believe in doing so, I've made the process of getting comfortable with fear feel less scary. This takes away some of your fear's power.

If you want honesty, vulnerability, lots of laughs, and the occasional kick in the pants to go for it, then this book is perfect for you.

Why Listen To Me?

Because I've taught myself how to go after the things I want most in my life, I didn't need to become fearless to do them.

Hold on. Let me backtrack and properly introduce myself.

My name is Monique Malcolm. I'm the founder of Take Tiny Action, where I help people use small action steps to propel them toward achieving their goals.

I've hiked a glacier in Iceland, taught myself graphic design, paid off more than $100,000 in debt, swam in a bioluminescent lagoon, chased the Northern Lights, created a planner system, and launched a successful podcast.

I've done all of those things, but I'm still not fearless. I feel afraid all of the time.

Honestly, most of those things might not have happened if it weren't for a life-altering event. On September 30, 2012, my brother Maurice was involved in a fatal motorcycle accident.

At the time of his death, Maurice's life seemed to be going in the right direction. He had goals. He had a great job. He'd put a deposit down on a condo and was excited to move in. He'd even bought a new car.

Suddenly, I was painfully aware that your time was up once

the lid was closed on your casket. I had been coasting through life, dragging around a big black garbage bag full of unfulfilled goals and dreams with a sprinkle of regret to top them off. I couldn't bear the thought of blowing my chance at living a full life by not trying to go after some of my dreams.

At the height of my grief, I wrote a list of incredible experiences, travel, plans, and milestone life goals. I put them on a page on my blog called *The Awesome List*. It was a space created to honor Maurice's memory and document my attempt at living a vibrant, fulfilling, and fun life. Then, slowly I started working to check things off of my list.

I've done things I believed I had to wait to do until I had more money, success, and a lot less fear. I now recognize that type of thinking for what it is: a limitation put in place by fear. And I understand that the person standing in my way saying, "You can't do that," was me.

In almost all of its forms, fear is a thief. It robs your life of joy and happiness. When you stop letting fear have all the fun, you take back your joy.

I found the courage and the boldness to stop letting fear have all the fun in my life. Best of all, I realized that I didn't need to be fearless to do it. The same is possible for you, and I will teach you how.

I'm ready to get this party started. Let's have some fun. Keep reading.

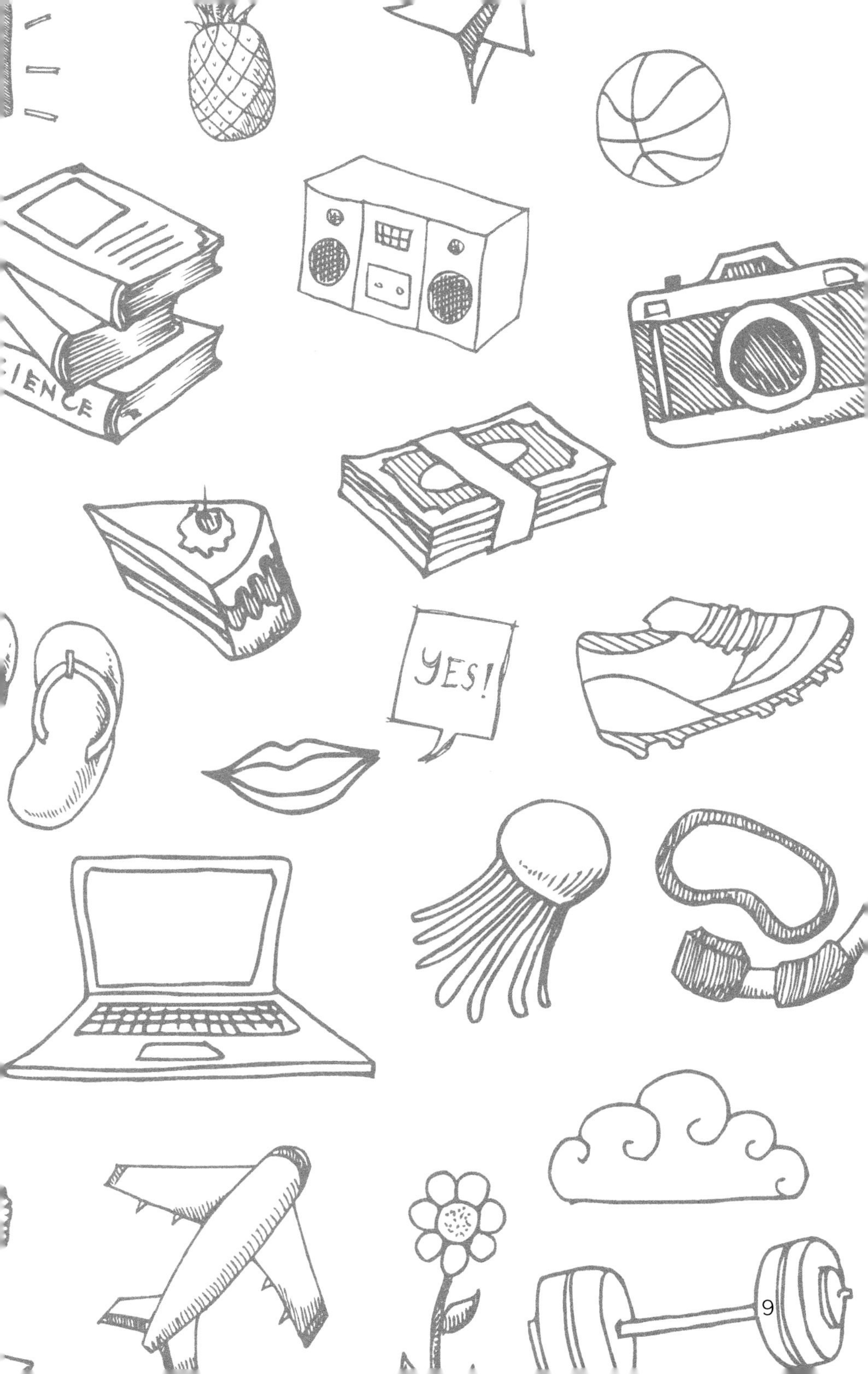
YES!

SCIENCE
YES!

ADVICE #1

A Life Built On Fear Already Has Built-In Limitations

"Pick a jelly bean."

You wouldn't think such a simple request could cause so much anxiety but trust me, it does. Whenever I teach one of my workshops about fear, I start by having the attendees take the BeanBoozled challenge.

BeanBoozled is a silly game from the makers of Jelly Belly that pairs two jelly beans that look alike but taste different. There are the usual popular flavors like Juicy Pear, Birthday Cake, and Tutti Frutti, and then there are wild flavors like Booger, Stinky Socks, and Rotten Egg. The catch is that you don't know which flavor you've picked until you take a bite. So you can see how choosing a single jelly bean can be nerve-racking.

I set cups of BeanBoozled jelly beans on the tables in front of the attendees and projected an image on the screen showing the possible flavors they could choose. Then, I wait.

Nervous laughter settles around the room. Some attendees

stare up at the projector screen in complete horror. At least one or two people pick up their cups, shake them, and peer intently at the jelly beans like that's going to reveal an answer. My favorites are the attendees who put on a brave face, pick a random jelly bean without much deliberation, and toss it in their mouths. Most attendees whisper amongst themselves about their potential choices while trying to justify the risk.

It sounds something like this, "Rotten Egg?! Dead Fish?! Ew. Maybe I should choose Berry Blue because the wild flavor is Toothpaste. Even Lime doesn't seem that bad because its wild flavor is Lawn Clippings. I think I can handle that."

I listen to this back-and-forth banter, amused, before instructing everyone to taste their jelly beans. More nervous laughter, giggles, and full-on belly laughs filled the room. I can tell who chose the right flavors instantly by the relief on their faces.

Unfortunately, many attendees are spitting their beans into their napkins or trash cans. This activity is my favorite way to break the ice and segue into the topic of fear, which can be heavy. It's also amusing to see which attendees get the Rotten Egg. That never gets old.

Fear can influence even the most minor, most insignificant decisions. Choosing a jelly bean is not a life-altering decision. Really, what's the worst that can happen? You pick a flavor. You bite into it. Realize it's a bad one. Make a face. Laugh. Throw it away and move on. However, the added risk and uncertainty of not knowing what flavor you've picked until you've tasted it sets off the alarm bells.

My workshop attendees typically fall into one of three categories of risk tolerance: thrill-seekers, medium-risk-takers, and zero-tolerance-risk-takers.

The thrill-seeker is fairly risk-tolerant. For them, taking the BeanBoozled challenge feels fun and thrilling. They'd probably try every jelly bean flavor if left to their own devices.

The medium-risk-taker is moderately risk-tolerant. For them, taking the challenge could go either way. They may accept the risk, choose a random jelly bean, or pick a safe flavor like Berry Blue.

The zero-tolerance risk-taker is risk-averse. They don't want to risk anything. The challenge is a nightmare scenario for them, so they don't participate.

Thrill-seekers and zero-tolerance-risk-takers are the least common attendees at my fear workshops. There's usually no more than one or two. The majority of people fall into the medium-risk-taker category. I suspect this is also the case for most people reading this book.

Leading those workshops taught me that a life built on a foundation of fear already has built-in limitations. Your life experiences will expand to fill the spaces not already inhabited by your fear. Too much fear causes your life experiences to contract because there isn't enough room for anything else. If you're already working against limitations out of fear, you're restricted from reaching your full potential before you begin.

Everyone Experiences Fear

I know I'm supposed to keep you in suspense and drag this out until you're further along in the book, but I'm not great at withholding surprises. My big secret about fear is that it is natural, and everyone experiences it.

Every human walking this big beautiful ball of water has had their fair share of fears. Those fears come in many shapes and sizes. Some fears have unique origin stories.

Take my sister Myria as an example. She fears her car door might open while she makes a sharp turn. A fear she now lives with because she fell out of the car when we were kids.

Other fears are entirely illogical. I think potato salad is evil. I dislike making eye contact with birds because they act unpredictably. It doesn't make much sense, but many of our fears don't.

Your fears are a lot like a mystery grab bag. You don't know what is inside until you tear open the bag and dump the contents on the table. Only then do you know if what you've received is something of value or if you ended up with somebody's overflow of unwanted junk.

Even though dealing with fear is a universal experience, the irony lies in that you weren't born a fearful being. Newborn babies come into the world bright-eyed, screaming with only two concerns: falling and loud noises. Over the years, as you developed, explored, and started to experience the world, your list of fears began to surface and take shape. Where you were once a fearless toddler diving off the couch and eating mud pies full of wriggling worms, you've transformed into a rational person concerned with self-preservation and doing your best to survive while toting around a hefty sack full of fears that you learned.

Most of these fears can fit into three categories: primal, rational, and irrational.

Primal fear is your body's physical response to danger. Your brain is a fantastic piece of machinery that ensures you respond effectively to life-or-death situations. It's like when Spiderman's spidey senses kick in to let him know that he's in harm's way. When that happens, your brain activates your "fight or flight" response alerting your body to prepare to defend itself or to run away.

Imagine what would happen if you didn't have primal fear to activate your "fight or flight" response as you crossed paths with a grizzly bear while hiking through the woods. You'd probably react incorrectly. You'd do something silly, like trying to hug the bear instead of turning in the other direction to flee.

While bears might look cute and furry like the Charmin Bear, don't be fooled, it's still a wild animal. Running away is an entirely acceptable response.

Thankfully your primal fear is always on standby and ready to alert you to the dangers of grappling with a bear. You get to live to see another day and the bear goes about his business unbothered, doing whatever it is that bears do—possibly stealing picnic baskets or getting their paws stuck in pots of honey.

Important Note: The primary role of fear is to keep you safe from danger. However, your primal fear response isn't sophisticated enough to tell the difference between fear caused by a bear attack or nonlethal threats to your overall well-being. That is where rational and irrational fears come into play.

Rational fear is based on something that could happen but isn't a threat or immediate danger. Some examples of rational fears are the fear of losing a small child in a crowded mall, not achieving your life goals, or losing people you love as they age. Each of these experiences could happen, but you can't predict if or when they will. Rational fears reflect our deepest concerns and worries in life.

Finally, there is irrational fear based on something hypothetical, not real, or that poses no actual danger. (Irrational fears can turn into phobias, but I'm not a psychologist, which goes beyond the scope of this book.) The thing about irrational fears is that they exist solely inside your mind. That means the only thing fueling your irrational fear is Y-O-U. You feed the fear, which allows it to get stronger.

When I talk about fear in this book, I'm referring to your irrational fears.

Irrational fear is the most insidious of the three types of fear because it limits your life experience in various ways. Fear feeds stagnation, keeps you stuck, and leads you to live a small life.

All your irrational fear needs is a tiny hint that you're about to try something risky before it begins to sound the alarm and protest loudly. Then comes a flood of well-intentioned excuses, reasons, stories, and justifications about why doing that thing is a bad idea.

All of this is done under the guise of keeping you safe. But really, it's your irrational fear acting like an overprotective parent. You've seen the type. The parent who won't let their children venture outside the fence to play with the neighborhood kids. So they keep them confined to the yard, convincing them it's for their own good. Meanwhile, the kids don't thrive. Instead, they learn to cope with their parent's stifling overreach by minimizing their desire to explore what lies beyond their backyard. This is precisely how the Chorus of Fear (more on this in just a minute) shows up in your life—trying to smother your ambitions with its overprotectiveness.

If left unchecked, those excuses become a part of a nagging chorus, like when a song you don't like gets stuck in your head all afternoon. "The Song That Never Ends" from **Lamb Chop's Play-Along** immediately comes to mind. For that reason, I call the voice of our irrational fears the Chorus of Fear.

The Chorus Of Fear Sings To Everyone

The Chorus of Fear is the voice in the back of your mind talking you out of taking risks, doing uncomfortable things, or trying something new. That voice holds you back, makes you feel small and insecure, and tries to have all of the fun at your expense.

The Chorus of Fear sings to everyone. It is masterful. Layering together a harmonious combination of excuses and justifications designed to minimize your ambitions. Everyone has a powerful action-stopping playlist of reasons (aka the hits) that the Chorus of Fear has turned into their "Greatest Hits." This playlist is unique and specific to you. Pulling source material from your insecurities, past experiences, hurts, and traumas.

The siren-like voice of the Chorus of Fear can be so seductive while singing your playlist of greatest hits that you wouldn't hesitate to walk away from a life-altering opportunity so that you could rest your head on the bosom of familiarity and comfort. This is an album that no one asked for, yet we all have one tucked away in the back of our mental shelves.

For instance, the Chorus of Fear likes spinning my excuses with lyrics like "What makes you think you can do that?" "It didn't work before, so it probably won't work this time." And my personal favorite is the classic hit, "That's not good enough. It needs to be perfect."

For you, lyrics like "I don't know where to start," "Nobody's going to buy that from me," "This is never going to work," or "What would people say?" may sound familiar. With little effort, you could probably add more hits to the list. The Chorus of Fear's greatest hit list is expansive. It puts *Now That's What I Call Music!* to shame.

I consider myself to be an optimist. I believe that things always work out eventually. Still, I recognize that it's wildly audacious to think that God (the universe or whatever higher power you believe in) will continue to grant you additional opportunities to do the things you are here to do. You aren't Super Mario. You can't exchange gold coins for extra lives to get this right. You only have one.

Regardless, the Chorus of Fear shows up daily to spin another convincing rendition of your greatest hits.

Create Your Greatest Hits Playlist

EXERCISE

You have a Greatest Hits playlist curated by the Chorus of Fear specifically for you. It features the perfect mix of excuses, reasons, and stories (aka the hits) to stop you from taking action. What would the song titles be for the top five hits on your playlist?

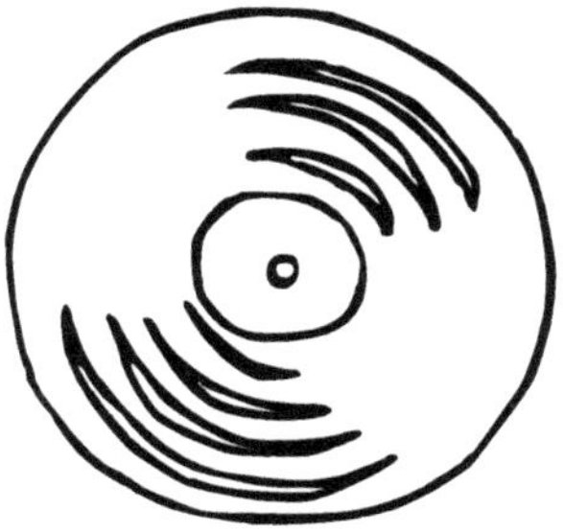

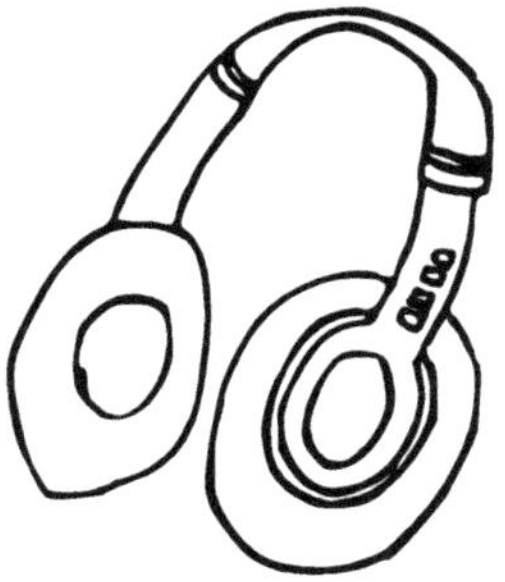

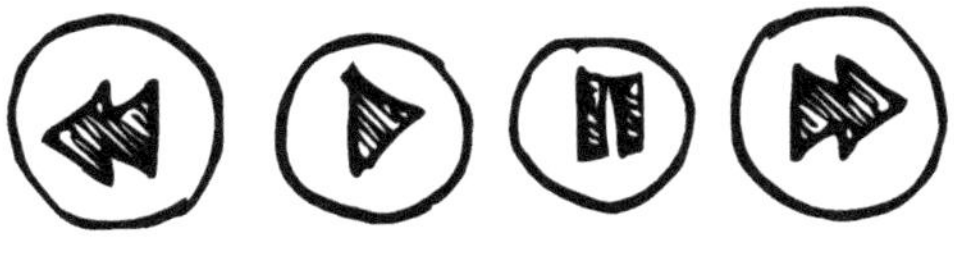

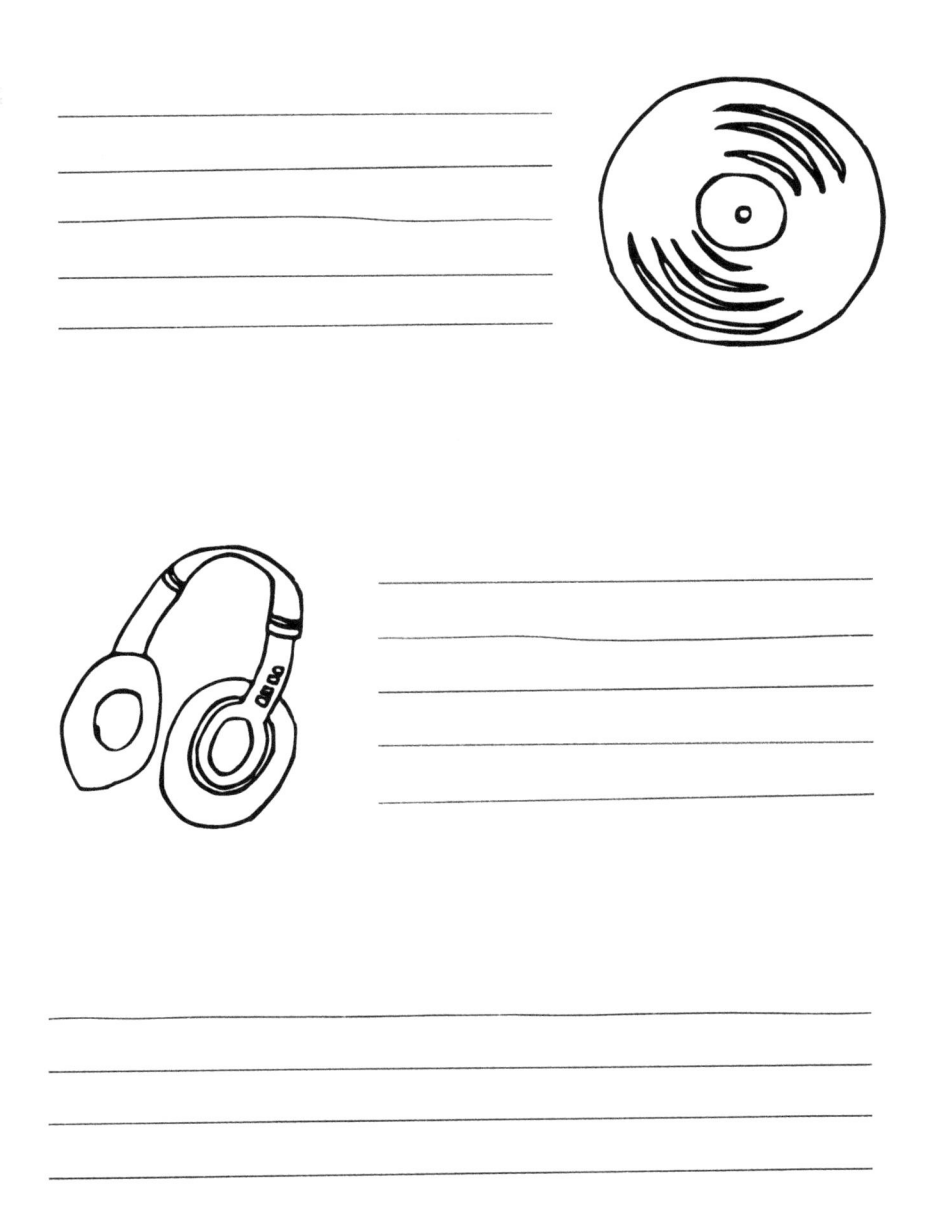

Taryn's Fear Fable

I was working a corporate job that everyone thought I was made for. I was doing phenomenally. I had an attractive salary. I had experience. I had a great team. But the job was eating away at my mental health.

I had a side business that made me happy. Financially, it scared me to think about leaving my job to work on it full-time.

In 2018, my husband and I decided we wanted to start trying for a family. I got pregnant. Unfortunately, that pregnancy ended in a miscarriage. This put us on a long journey of infertility.

Honestly, that helped me push past the fear at that point—losing that pregnancy and figuring out how to show up for a job when you are feeling torn apart, emotionally and mentally. I was going through so many things. I knew that I needed to focus on myself.

I could have left sooner, but the fear weighed on me. What if it doesn't work out? What are people going to think? What if my husband resents me because I left this cushy salary for something I felt passionate about, and now I'm not contributing similarly? What if I never get pregnant again? What if it's because my body is so stressed? Or what if I do, and I'm not able to be a present mom because I'm overwhelmed by my job? There were a lot of different narratives playing in my head.

Even though it was a difficult season for me, I think it positively affected my decisions later. I was able to take that fear and decide to put myself and our future first. The job was getting in the way of a better path for me as a human.

There were a lot of feelings. That's when things changed from "I'm so scared of this" to "No matter what that fear looks like, I have to do this because it's way scarier to think of what happens if I don't."

Taryn Jerez

The Levels Of Apprehension

No one is exempt from feeling the influence of the Chorus of Fear. I've spent quite a bit detailing how the Chorus of Fear likes to show up, but let's discuss how to measure its influence.

I developed a scale called The Chorus of Fear's Levels of Apprehension. The Levels of Apprehension measure the amount of fear or anxiety you experience when you are thinking about taking some action. There are three levels: the Warm Up, the Rehearsal, and the Performance.

Level One: The Warm Up

At the onset of an event or something with an uncertain outcome, you immediately enter Level One: the Warm Up. The Warm Up is like a mental mic check. At this level, you hear the Chorus of Fear's early excuses step up and sing into the mic.

Mic check. Mic check. Is this thing on?

This is the voice that stage whispers, "I don't know how to do this." "This seems too hard." "I can't afford it." "I'm not good at that." "I don't want to say anything and bother them." You say these little statements to yourself so often—each one eats away at your confidence. Planting just enough seeds of doubt to make you question your resolve to continue forward.

For you, the Warm Up might sound like the voice of your parents warning you against looking for a new job because "You already have a good job."

For me, it often feels like overthinking or a steady stream of additional questions. Mentally I hear the Chorus of Fear say, "What about this?" and "Oh yeah… Don't forget about that." It's a loop that distracts me from deciding to move forward.

Level Two: The Rehearsal

If you don't get your fear in check during the Warm Up, you move up to the Rehearsal. During the Rehearsal, the Chorus of Fear gets louder and more persistent with its excuses. It narrows down the list of your Greatest Hits and solidifies the playlist.

An easy way to recognize that you are in the Rehearsal is by paying attention to how fear is showing up.

Imagine you're in a choir rehearsal but with various manifestations of your fear whirling around. You have Resistance off to one side practicing scales. Perfectionism is warmed up and ready to go. Procrastination is in the back, harmonizing with distractions. Meanwhile, Overwhelmed and Stressed are practicing their solo acts. They all sound amazing.

For you, the Rehearsal might sound like "I'll get to that next week" or "I don't have enough experience."

For me, it often feels like self-sabotage, which is knowing what you need to do to achieve your goal and doing things that conflict with your ability to reach them. Like the time I spent six months paying for a personal trainer to help me get into the best shape of my life. I saw results at the end of our time together but not the results I would have experienced if I had followed her advice to clean up my diet. Instead, I indulged in too many sweets, then held my breath and prayed every time I had to take new measurements. I actively worked against myself because I resisted making the necessary changes.

The Rehearsal stage is critical because you are at a pivotal do or don't moment. If you can push through your feelings of discomfort, you can walk yourself back down to the Warm Up stage. But if you're still unable to quiet the Chorus of Fear, you enter the final Level of Apprehension, the Performance.

Level Three: The Performance

Have you ever been to a Beyoncé concert? If not, let me paint you a picture; if you have, you know what I'm talking about.

Beyoncé's concerts are an experience with a capital E. The music is blaring, the lights are flashing, and the crowd is excited. Everyone is waiting for Beyoncé to come on stage. Suddenly and without warning, the lights dim, the music gets louder, and you think you see a shadowy figure rising out of the center of the stage. The crowd grows more agitated. You can feel the electricity of everyone's energy in the air. In a flash, the spotlight clicks on, your eyes adjust, and then you see Queen Bey in all of her regal glory, posed in her glittering sequined leotard and six-inch stiletto boots. The crowd erupts. Everyone is screaming and losing their minds. Finally, the queen has arrived—the beat drops. You hold your breath for half a second before Beyoncé belts out her first note. Your brain explodes, and you have a brief out-of-body experience.

The whole thing sounds pretty epic, right?

Right. Except it is not Beyoncé strutting across the stage in six-inch stiletto boots; it is the Chorus of Fear. The Chorus of Fear is putting on a stellar performance for one in the confines of your mind. It has assembled a well-rehearsed setlist and is running through your greatest hits like a seasoned pro.

Because the Chorus of Fear is giving a Beyoncé-level performance, your anxiety is sky-high. You feel nauseous. You no longer believe that 'going for it' is a good idea. It's the worst idea that you can think of. Now you're convincing yourself that you didn't want to achieve that goal. You pack away your desire and tell yourself it's better this way. You let fear have all the fun.

The Performance stage sucks! It becomes like The Song That Never Ends when you let the Chorus of Fear sing unchecked for too long. And it goes on and on, my friend. The same lines looped over and over again with no end. What's worse is that you don't even like that song. No matter how hard you try to shake it loose or replace it with another song, you just have to let it run its course. But the running doesn't stop.

Fear has a way of making you contract into yourself. Instead of being a big juicy grape hanging on the vine of life, you become shriveled and dried out like a raisin. That's not what I want for you, my succulent little cotton candy grape. I don't want you to shrink; I want you to expand.

The presence of the Chorus of Fear does not mean you should give up on achieving your dreams, taking risks, or making bold plans.

Being fearless is not a prerequisite to living a big full life.

From this point forward, your mission, should you accept it, is to turn down the volume on the Chorus of Fear's singing long enough to take the next small step. Baby steps are perfect.

Best of all, I'm here to teach you how. The coming chapters cover practical yet actionable steps you can take well before the Chorus of Fear makes it to that Beyoncé-esque Performance stage.

ADVICE #1

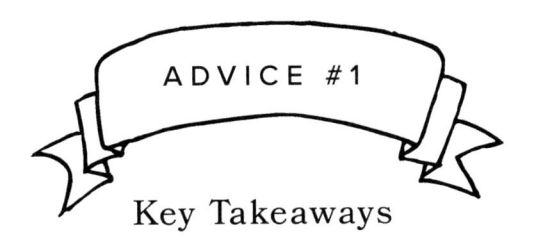

Key Takeaways

1. Your life expands to fill the space not occupied by fear. Working against limitations created out of fear restricts you from reaching your full potential.

2. The primary role of fear is to keep you safe. Unfortunately, your primal fear response can't tell the difference between fear caused by actual danger or an imagined threat.

3. The Chorus of Fear is the internal voice talking you out of taking risks and going after your dreams. It curates a perfect playlist full of excuses, reasons, and stories (aka the hits) to stop you from taking action.

4. The Levels of Apprehension measure the amount of fear or anxiety you experience when you are thinking about taking some type of action.

5. You don't need to be fearless to live a great life.

The Chorus Of Fear's Levels Of Apprehension

The amount of fear or anxiety you experience when thinking about taking action.

THE WARM-UP	**THE REHEARSAL**	**THE PERFORMANCE**
A mental mic check. The Chorus of Fear is warming up by singing an excuse or two.	The Chorus of Fear has narrowed down your Greatest Hits list of excuses and is starting to weave them into a playlist.	Like opening night at a Beyoncé concert. The Chorus of Fear has curated your perfect Greatest Hits playlist and is running through it flawlessly.
This could look like:	**This could look like:**	**This could look like:**
A whispering internal voice saying, "This seems too hard."	A persistent internal voice saying, "I don't have enough experience" or "I'll get to that next week"	A loud, forceful internal voice saying, "I can't do this" or "It will never work. Why bother".
The excuses and reasons are subtle, like, "I don't know how to do this," instead of loud or forceful.	Resistance shows up in the form of perfectionism, procrastination, and distractions.	A constant creeping sense of anxiety, dread or overwhelm.
You start overthinking.	The Chorus of Fear is louder and more persistent with its excuses and stories.	A nagging chorus of excuses that feel reasonable and compelling.
	You're at a pivotal "Do-or-don't" moment.	You give up or no longer try to take action.

EXERCISE

Think about a recent situation where you felt afraid, and the Chorus of Fear showed up. Which level did you find yourself at?

28

ADVICE #2:

Make Sure You Understand The True Cost Of Listening To Fear

Once, as I left the gym, I had a revealing conversation with a gym buddy. He was one of those extremely fit guys with massive arms. I had been consistent with my workout routine for a while, so I jokingly but seriously asked him to be my trainer. I told him my goal was to have abs by my birthday in December.

Without missing a beat, he looked me straight in the eye and laughed. (That wasn't awkward or anything.) Then, he said something along the lines of, "I don't like training people because nobody wants to work. They quit when it gets hard."

Frowning and offended, I made a face at him. We were both gym regulars at that point. We had crossed paths multiple times a week for months. How could he not see my readiness to commit to my fitness goal? I tried convincing him, but I proved his point with the following words out of my mouth. "How much cake would I be able to eat under your fitness plan?"

Please don't laugh. Cake is my weakness.

My question drew even more laughter. He might have even shed a tear or two. That's when he said these magic words to me, "The thing about having abs is you can't bargain your way into getting them. You have to be willing to be uncomfortable. Which do you want? Do you want the comfort of eating cake, or do you want abs?"

I thought he was crazy. Of course, I could have cake! I went to the gym regularly. I busted my butt doing multiple forms of acceptable torture framed as fitness moves like burpees and push-ups. I was sure I could have both.

It took several months for me to understand the truth in his statement. I'd hit the gym as a part of my usual routine, but I made zero progress on my abs goal. The scale wasn't budging either. I hadn't made any changes to the way that I ate. Even though I said out loud that I wanted abs, my actions showed that I chose cake.

Finally, frustrated with my lack of progress, I made a few changes. I hate to admit this, but I gave up the cake. To be fair, I also cut out other sweets like candy and processed sugars. After a few months, I saw the outline of two cute baby abs peeking through my compression tights.

Our conversation that day changed the shape of my beliefs. So I guess that super-buff gym guy was right. I had to choose. I could have the abs, but I had to be willing to get uncomfortable to get them.

I wasn't afraid to give up the cake. Cake isn't scary. I was afraid of the discomfort of giving up something I found comforting and not knowing if that loss would be worth it. I was fearful that I'd disappoint myself because even though I chose abs, I'd keep backsliding and finding myself with a mouth full of cake. I was afraid of the possibility that despite my best efforts, I still might not reach my goal. The Chorus of Fear filled my head with so many excuses that I only focused on avoiding my discomfort over the loss of cake instead of seeing what I could gain.

And therein lies one of the many problems we face when listening to the Chorus of Fear, trying to avoid feeling uncomfortable to the point of choosing short-term comfort over long-term gain. Our need to feel comfortable becomes the silent killer of our dreams, plans, and ideas.

What are you currently putting off doing or acting on because the Chorus of Fear has convinced you it was too uncomfortable? Making an important decision about a significant relationship? Putting a deposit down on your dream vacation? Joining a karate class? Confronting your credit card debt? Moving across the country?

Whatever it is, the Chorus of Fear causes you to do unnecessary mental gymnastics in justification for not taking the action you know you need to take. That clever voice in your head always wants to keep you small, safe, and comfortable. Your fear stops you from taking the action necessary to get what you want out of life. Once you get honest with yourself about what you're putting off because of fear, you have an essential decision to make: do it and change or do nothing and remain the same. The rest of this chapter is an eye-opening look at the hidden costs of letting fear have all the fun.

Get Comfortable With Being Uncomfortable

Fear causes a lot of uncomfortable feelings: overwhelm, anxiety, anger, and sadness, just to name a few. Whether you realize it or not, you actively or passively seek comfort. You make dozens of daily decisions to preserve your baseline level of comfort.

As far as the Chorus of Fear is concerned, comfortable equals safe. If you're comfortable, you aren't experiencing feelings of distress. You aren't anxious. You aren't in a state of panic. And since keeping you safe is the primary job of fear, it tries to do so at all costs, even if that means derailing your attempts to live a bolder life.

Your need for comfort is the Chorus of Fear's greatest ally because your desire to avoid discomfort sustains it.

Life is full of opportunities to be uncomfortable. There is no shortage of uncomfortable experiences or situations you can find yourself in. For instance, asking someone on a date without guaranteeing that you won't be turned down can be uncomfortable. Going to a new church or house of worship for the first time can be uncomfortable. Trying a new food from a different culture can be uncomfortable too.

The truth about comfort that many people fail to realize is there is discomfort in taking a risk, but there is also discomfort in choosing not to act because of fear. When you don't go after what you want because of fear, you only protect yourself in the short term. You can temporarily avoid uncomfortable feelings like embarrassment, disappointment, or rejection. What you don't think about is how giving into your fears for temporary relief opens the door to problems later.

You're trading in short-term relief for long-term discomfort.

That's one of the hidden costs of listening to the Chorus of Fear. You end up paying the price because you are carrying unrealized desires.

The Chorus of Fear does not want you to grow to reach your full potential. After all, growth is painful, and the pain feels uncomfortable. It's like lifting weights at the gym. Your muscles must be stretched and torn consistently to grow. You experience the growth and repair process as pain and discomfort.

Meanwhile, your body rebuilds the muscle larger and stronger. Growth is destructive. You can't have growth without pain. That's why you need to get comfortable with being uncomfortable.

Being bold enough to live the life you want involves pain. It will stretch and challenge you. Taking action in the face of fear will force you to be stronger. I won't sugarcoat it. If you continue on this journey of not allowing fear to have all the fun, you will get battered and bruised on occasion. You will fall, rip your jeans, and skin your knees. You will become uncomfortable.

If the realization hasn't dawned on you, **you will not be comfortable 100% of your life**. I can promise you that.

Understanding how taking risks and going after things you want causes discomfort is relatively straightforward. It's equally vital that you recognize your discomfort from not doing what you want. You have to decide which of those discomforts feels worse. Would you rather be uncomfortable pushing through fear to go after your dreams or deal with the regret and other potential consequences of not taking that risk?

You get to choose your level of discomfort.

It's a choice that only you can make. So my advice to you is to determine what that short-term comfort costs. Decide whether or not you accept that cost. Then, get comfortable with being uncomfortable.

Listening To The Chorus Of Fear Takes A Toll

We tend to believe that not making a decision or moving forward means no harm is being done, but that's not true. Listening to the Chorus of Fear has a cost and takes a toll. Do you know how much you're paying?

Letting fear be the driver of your decisions is like taking the expressway toll roads along the highway of your life. You barely register the tolls that you're paying. You see the signs that a toll booth is coming up, but you don't stop to think about the cost. You just pay for it.

Seventy-five cents here. One dollar and twenty-five cents there. Fifty cents here. Another two dollars. Those debits seem small, but throughout your life, they add up.

Giving in to the Chorus of Fear's excuses takes a toll on your life. Those transactions are charged to you and debited directly from your life's essence. Unlike actual toll booths, there are no reloadable toll passes.

Your life is finite.

If you encounter enough tolls, eventually, you'll find yourself scrounging around in the cup holder seeking change. By then, it might be too late.

It's laughable that the Chorus of Fear dares to charge for its service (the one you didn't ask for), and you receive no benefit. Don't let the Chorus of Fear take its toll. The price you pay for letting fear drive your decisions shows up in the form of a physical, emotional, or financial toll. Sometimes it's all three.

PHYSICAL TOLLS

Physical tolls put a strain on your physical well-being. Your body's physical response to fear stimulates your nervous system to release hormones like cortisol and adrenaline. These hormones are critical components of your "fight or flight" reaction when you're in imminent danger, but they're less useful when dealing with abstract threats like failing a test.

Living in a state of constant fear weakens your immune system. This physically affects your body, causing sleep, memory, digestion, blood pressure, and other issues.

EMOTIONAL TOLLS

Emotional tolls put a strain on your emotional state of mind. The disruption to your emotional state can cause problems related to anxiety disorder, anger issues, sadness, stress, and other unpleasant emotions.

Emotional tolls can develop when you don't at least try to go after what you want. Your unmet desires plus lack of fulfillment lead to rumination, which paves the way for regret. This is why regret is one of the most commonly experienced emotional tolls.

I stumbled on a great example of an emotional toll while giving a presentation. I asked attendees to share something they wanted but hadn't done because fear kept getting in the way. Two women raised their hands and said they wanted to write and publish books. One of the women shared that writing a book had been her dream her entire life. The other woman shared that she had already written four books but hadn't published one.

She had four books trapped in the digital dungeon of her computer because the Chorus of Fear made her believe she'd be more comfortable if she didn't publish them. Not publishing those books didn't remove the desire. It didn't make her feel better in the long term. She was still uncomfortable. It made me wonder what emotional toll she has paid over the years because carrying the unrealized potential of four books is heavy.

FINANCIAL TOLLS

Financial tolls put a strain on your finances. Your fear impacts your money by making you hesitant to change your financial situation. The Chorus of Fear is perfectly skilled at fabricating why you shouldn't seek a promotion. It makes you lack confidence in understanding money matters, like investing in the stock market.

Unfortunately, it doesn't stop there. Listening to fear can prevent you from regaining control of your finances.

For years, I tried to convince myself that my financial situation wasn't shakier than a game of Jenga. Every month I paid the minimum balances on multiple credit cards and my student loans while sheepishly glancing at the total balances owed. I was in six-figure debt and afraid to face the fact that years of poor money habits weighed down my life. Ashamed, I buried my head in the sand and continued to do nothing about addressing the debt that I'd accumulated.

Here's a little gummy worm to chew on:

Doing nothing is an action and a decision. It's not a neutral decision.

I believed that doing nothing to reel in my debt was a decision free from consequences and repercussions. That wasn't true. I was stressing about money which triggered periods of insomnia, waking me in the middle of the night. I racked up interest charges month after month. I lived paycheck to paycheck while carrying around a barrel of guilt and shame. I hit the trifecta of paying a physical, emotional, and financial toll.

Did ignoring my money problems erase the consequences of the situation I was afraid to face? Nope! It changed nothing. The only thing my inaction did was cause more misery.

Not making a decision has consequences.

You can't stay in limbo forever. You can't straddle the fence. It's better to exercise choice, make your decision and take a leap of faith versus having God (the Universe or insert the higher power you believe in), someone else, or inconvenient circumstances force you into action. Eventually, something has to give, and it will be given by choice or taken by force. Trust me, it is better to choose. The outcome is almost always better when you get to decide for yourself.

Most of the time, you don't recognize the cost of listening

to the Chorus of Fear. The price you pay is greater and more painful than the actual feelings of fear. Physical, emotional, and financial tolls are the unaccounted-for costs of letting fear have all the fun.

Carrying the weight of unfulfilled desires, goals, and dreams is heavy. Those burdens cause wear and tear not only on your mental state but your physical body too. Your inaction ends up being more costly than you planned.

What discomfort have you found yourself in by letting fear take its toll?

Life's Toll Booth

The Chorus of Fear's Toll Booth

The price you pay for listening to your fear. It's possible to pay all three tolls at the same time.

PHYSICAL TOLLS:	EMOTIONAL TOLLS:	FINANCIAL TOLLS:
Put a strain on your physical well-being	Put a strain on your emotional state	Put a strain on your financial situation
This could cause:	This could cause:	This could cause:
Weakening of your immune system	Unpleasant emotions like anger, sadness, and anxiety	Missed opportunities to advance in your career
Problems with sleep, memory, digestion, or blood pressure	Constant rumination over risks you've decided not to take	Financial instability
	Feelings of regret	

EXERCISE

Listening to the Chorus of Fear always comes at a cost. You pay those costs as physical, emotional, or financial tolls on your life. Think of a situation where you decided not to take action because you listened to your fear. What was the cost of that inaction? Which tolls did you end up paying?

_____
_____
_____
_____
_____
_____
_____
_____
_____
_____
_____
_____
_____
_____
_____
_____

Elizabeth's Fear Fable

I've always enjoyed being a funny person. I enjoy making people laugh. But when it comes time to do something more like writing out a set to test at a comedy club, I'm paralyzed. Where do I start? What if I'm not good at comedy? What if people don't laugh?

Once, someone offered me a part in a comedic play. They were like, "We saw you perform your poetry. I think you'd be great at this. You should come to my studio and try out for this play."

I never followed up on that. I was too paralyzed by the fear of what would happen next. What would people say? What would my family say if they heard me talking a certain way?

I wish that I had taken the opportunity and done the play. What would that have led to if I had said yes to that one thing? Maybe I would have learned I'm a funny friend, but I'm not that funny. Or perhaps I am. I think that would have been an interesting experience. I'm sad that I never took them up on that offer.

Elizabeth Fening

Decisions Have A Ripple Effect

Nobody benefits from your being held hostage by fear.

What do you get out of not going for it? Nothing. How does your family benefit from you not going for it? They don't. No one benefits, yet that doesn't prevent them from being impacted.

Your decisions don't only affect you. I want you to start considering how far the impact of not trying can reach. There's a chance the effects of your decision don't extend beyond you, but there's the real possibility that by choosing the safe option, you're limiting the potential of others. When you stop to think about this, it blows your mind.

When my grandfather Joseph Malcolm decided to start his trucking company, J.N. Malcolm & Sons, there was no way for him to know the impact of that decision. All he knew for sure was that he wanted to start a business. So that's what he did. He began with a single dump truck and grew the company to 26 dump trucks, an office building, a mechanic's workshop, two front-end loaders, six BobCats, and other pieces of excavating equipment. J.N. Malcolm & Sons became one of the largest minority-owned trucking companies.

Imagine what could have happened if my grandfather had listened to the Chorus of Fear and didn't start that company? His fear would have impacted the careers of his truck drivers and staff. Over the life of his business, my grandfather employed hundreds of people. A few of them have started their own companies in the trucking industry. His three sons each currently own or have owned dump trucks. And three of his grandchildren work in the trucking industry.

I often think about my grandfather's decision to start a business and the impact that it has had on my family. His decision to push past his fear has had a ripple effect that still positively impacts people today.

What is listening to your fear costing you? Money is probably your go-to answer, but I challenge you to think beyond the dollar signs. There are important things at stake.

Start Viewing Your Fear As An Opportunity

In my experience, the thing you fear doing is usually the thing you most need to do. Fear is ironic like that. You interpret your feelings of unease and discomfort to mean stop or don't do it. In reality, your fear is like a big flashing neon sign pointing out what to focus on next.

Try looking at your fear from a fresh perspective. Would you like to experience growth? Are you willing to try? Step into your fear. Embrace those uncomfortable feelings. Move forward with courage.

Start viewing your fear as an opportunity. An opportunity to grow. A chance to change. An opportunity to find the courage to set yourself free. Fear is meant to make you pause, examine how you've been moving through the world and consider taking risks.

Finally, I've proved that the Chorus of Fear is overprotective and wants to convince you to choose the comfortable option at all times, but being comfortable can also be synonymous with playing small.

You grow by playing bigger.

You learn to push through the uncomfortable feelings of fear by experiencing them. The more you do it, the more you grow. Every time you grow, you raise the bar on your tolerance for fear. You grow by taking more risks; not taking risks stunts your growth. It reduces future life opportunities. Your ability to live a vibrant life is stifled by accepting your smallness and refusing to venture outside your comfort zone. Playing it safe doesn't lead to your intended result of living a great life.

When you experience fear, it is an opportunity to grow. Don't squander those opportunities.

Alisha's Fear Fable

I have always loved writing. I was the nerdy kid who liked doing book reports. I was a shy child, and even though I loved writing, I never told anyone. I never let anyone read what I was writing. That in itself was scary.

In elementary school, right around the fourth or fifth grade, I wanted to start a newsletter for our school. It was in the nineties, so I'm talking about a paper newsletter.

I remember being afraid until I told one of my friends. She encouraged me to ask our teacher. At the time, I didn't think my teacher was friendly. Eventually, I let my friend talk me into it. To my surprise, my teacher was all for it. She even volunteered to stay after school with us to work on it.

She helped us outline and write the newsletter while she edited it. When the newsletter launched, we went to the other classes to hand it out. There was a moment where I was like, "Oh, this is scary." Then I realized it was not that bad because I saw people talking about my work. They liked it, and I got terrific feedback.

Now I think about how taking that one step eased me into sharing my writing. I wrote for my high school and college newspaper which eventually led to me starting a blog and a podcast. I feel like it was that one little push past the fear that set me up to feel comfortable using my gifts and sharing my stories.

Alisha Robinson

ADVICE #2

Key Takeaways

1. Our need to feel comfortable is the biggest threat to our goals or aspirations. Be careful not to trade short-term relief for long-term discomfort.

2. Listening to the Chorus of Fear comes at a cost. The price is paid as a physical, emotional, or financial toll on our lives. Sometimes it's all three.

3. Inaction is both a decision and a choice. Decisions aren't neutral. They can have a positive or negative impact that impacts other people.

4. Learn to view fear as an opportunity for growth. It's often a sign signaling what to focus on next.

SCIENCE
YES!

ADVICE #3:

Name Your Fears And Take Back Your Power

Can I share a secret with you?

I was afraid to write this book.

As a writer, I realize this is a crazy thing to reveal. My job is to write. It's literally in my title. Logically I knew I could write a book. I possessed the skills. I had an idea. The desire was there. I had even written a tiny book previously. But none of that prevented the Chorus of Fear from showing up and blocking my creative flow.

Another thing you must understand about the Chorus of Fear is that it does not operate on logic. It runs on emotion. Feelings are its fuel of choice. And I had a lot of big feelings about writing this book.

My fear took on a completely irrational thought pattern. I worried about the future outcome of this book well before I even finished writing the first chapter. Not wanting to miss an opportunity to remind me of the "dangers" of putting myself out there, the Chorus of Fear showed up to my early writing sessions with a carefully curated playlist of my greatest hits that it played on a loop.

In my head, the Chorus of Fear sounded very similar to this:

"I don't know how to write a book."

"Where am I going to find enough words to fill a book?"

"How am I writing a book about fear when I'm still afraid to do so many things?"

"What if this book doesn't live up to the hype I've created?"

"No one is going to read this book."

"You're going to get poor reviews on Amazon."

If feelings help fuel the Chorus of Fear, mine was like an oil tanker. A constant fuel source allowed my mind's out-of-control fire to burn brighter. It wasn't enough for me to simply sit down and write. If we're being honest, that should have been easy. All I had to do was spill my thoughts, experiences, and insights onto the page. Right?

Nope! While under the influence of fear, I convinced myself that my writing had to be perfect. It needed to be flawless and able to transcend criticism. How else would I write an extraordinary New York Times bestseller that measured up to the writing of all my favorite authors and provided readers with a mind-blowing transformational experience?

Those irrational thoughts twisted and distorted my feelings so much that I felt blocked. How could I write this book? Was I expert enough? My self-imposed writing expectations were so unrealistic and impossibly high that I'm unsure if even the late great Maya Angelou could meet them. Fear was having all the fun.

When I found myself battling resistance, dealing with procrastination, and skipping multiple days of writing altogether, I knew I had to sort out my feelings to get to the root of my fear. I grabbed my journal and my favorite pen, and in the first line, I wrote, "I am afraid." Then, I asked myself why. I let my thoughts and feelings pour out onto the page. Many mirrored the Chorus of Fear's playlist explicitly curated for this writing project. But they mainly highlighted that I felt unsure about what would happen after this book was published. Would people like it? The Chorus of Fear, being what it is, filled the gaps in my imagination created by that uncertainty.

Something is compelling about being able to name your problem and write it down. The Chorus of Fear's grip on us begins to loosen when we become aware of our fear and acknowledge that we are feeling afraid.

For me, getting thoughts out of my head and onto paper is beneficial. Writing those thoughts and feelings down rather than letting them swirl in my head helps me process them. I can make sense of them. The simple act of writing allows me to put distance between myself and my fear. I can look at my thoughts and feelings objectively without the weight of them pressing down on me. It's like solving a word problem. I dig through the clues provided by my feelings to find a solution.

Here are some of the questions I like to ask myself:

"Are these thoughts irrational?"

"Do I believe this, or is the Chorus of Fear influencing these thoughts?"

"What can I do right now to feel less overwhelmed?"

"How would I move forward if I wasn't afraid?"

Uncovering a way forward sends a wave of relief washing over me because I face my fear head-on instead of letting it hold me back.

Fear causes unwanted feelings—big fears and those little fears too.

For example, you may notice that driving somewhere for the first time causes a tiny spark of fear. Your body tenses up. The roads are unfamiliar. You check the GPS and try to find the best route. Your hands feel sweaty on the steering wheel. Once you make it to your destination, you feel relieved. This is one of the many small fears we encounter daily.

I can teach you dozens of strategies and tricks for overcoming your fear, but you can't be empowered to take it back until you acknowledge that you have relinquished your power to fear.

The first step that you must take to stop fear from having all the fun is to acknowledge that you are afraid. This is simple but often avoided because we don't like to confront our uncomfortable feelings. Having awareness and owning our challenges allows us to change. And change usually invites discomfort to tag along.

Acknowledging your fear doesn't need to be a big thing. It doesn't require any 12-step meetings. You don't have to overthink it or buy a fancy journal to write in (although feel free to process your feelings on paper if that's useful for you). It is enough to say "I feel afraid" out loud or to yourself. That's it! All your acknowledgment has to be is you expressing awareness that fear has arrived and is chiming in on your decisions. Unfortunately, many people miss this step because they ignore their feelings.

While neglecting your feelings seems like a good strategy, it only works as a short-term solution. Shoving your feelings aside doesn't make them go away. You can't ghost your emotions, and you shouldn't try to. Not dealing with your feelings provides the fuel that sustains the fire. Without intervention, the fire will eventually consume you whole.

When you become aware that you are under the influence of your fear, you put yourself back in the driver's seat. You have choices. Do you take the risk? Will you try? Or do you not want to risk it? Having options empowers you to take control of your life.

Thinking back to my earlier book writing sessions, I realized I was letting fear drive the car. It was steering me further away from my intended destination, and I was at a crossroads. I had to make a choice. Was I willing to kick fear out of the driver's seat, take back control, and keep writing? Or was I going to let fear have all the fun and stop writing? I decided not to give another minute of fun to the Chorus of Fear. I chose to keep writing, but I had to dig deep to figure out exactly what I was afraid of.

You might find yourself at similar crossroads every day.

Do I apply for my dream college out-of-state? Or do I apply to my safety-net school that is local?

Do I take a pottery class this weekend, even though I've never tried it and might not be good at it? Or do I use the money for another dinner and a movie weekend?

Do I go to Megan's surprise party, even though I will know no one else there? Or do I stay home where it's quiet and I don't have to make small talk?

Decisions. Decisions. Decisions. There are many to make.

Fear is like the frenemy (friend + enemy) in TV sitcoms. They're always there in the background, annoyingly poking their head in the room and commenting when you did not ask their opinion. But you can't shut them down entirely because, occasionally, their unsolicited advice comes in handy.

Amber's Fear Fable

I was in college and dating a man who was a celebrity bodyguard. I use the term dating kind of loosely. He was busy, and I was in school. One day he invited me to go to the Bahamas. His client was going on vacation for a few days. It wasn't a long time.

I wanted to go. I thought it would be fun, but I was afraid to go. I was scared because I was raised to believe that if a man does something for you, he wants something in return. So I turned down that invitation.

He was shocked. He really couldn't believe it, like, You're not going to go?" And I said, "Yeah, no, I'm not going to go." Even though I wanted to, I was afraid.

Now 20 years later, I regret that decision. Not dramatically, but I think I should've just gone. Then I would have a different story to tell my kids about when I went on vacation to the Bahamas with a man I was seeing who worked for one of the biggest R&B stars.

That's what I think happens when we let fear get in the way of things. It keeps us from experiences that create memories that add color to our lives.

Amber Wright

Investigate What's At The Root Of Your Fear

Since I'm confessing my secrets and fears, here is another.

For a large part of my life, I've felt insecure about my height. Without shoes, I stand a hair over six feet tall. My height is supposed to be a blessing, but in my experience, a tall woman is seen as a freak of nature.

The teasing started in elementary school. Middle school was more of the same. The high school years were the worst. I've been called every not-so-clever nickname. I'd be impressed if you could think of a name I haven't been called.

The irony is that I was okay with my height within the confines of my home and family. Being tall isn't an anomaly. All of my family is above average height. I'm not even the tallest person (although I am the tallest girl). My dad always spoke as if being tall was an advantage. I couldn't understand how being constantly stared at and asked questions about my height could be advantageous to anyone.

All of that teasing taught me one thing...to shrink myself. I didn't want to be seen. I didn't want people to notice my height. I dressed in a way that didn't attract attention. I didn't wear heels. When I entered a room, I'd look at the floor and try my best to fade into the background. I didn't want to be judged.

Somewhere along the way, I picked up the belief that if I were the smartest, the best student, and the perfect daughter, I would be above criticism. I would be perfect. No one would have anything unkind to say, and it would spare me from their constant judgment. What would there be left to say if I did everything perfectly? Only positive things, right?

Achievement became a measure of my self-worth. And it turns out that is the exact recipe for perfectionism.

Aiming for perfection is a constant losing battle. What is perfect? How do you measure that? Better yet, how do you meet the standards demanded by perfection? The bar is so high, and it only goes higher, never lower.

Trying to be perfect didn't change anything. It didn't make the kids less harsh. It didn't deter strangers from commenting on my height. But it did do one thing... increase my sensitivity to criticism.

I deeply feared being judged for my shortcomings (or what others perceived as a shortcoming like my height). I always felt like, at any moment, someone would burst my bubble and point out my flaws. Then, the world would discover the truth: I wasn't intelligent, funny, or loveable. I was just a tall freak. Creating a reality where people saw me as knowledgeable, my work as excellent, and praised my accomplishments was how I shielded myself from the discomfort of their judgment.

The Two Levels Of Fear

We experience fear at two levels: on the surface and deeply rooted within our minds.

Surface Fears

Surface fears are influenced by the situations in your life. You can think of them as your everyday fears. They are the fears you experience when you need to make a decision, try something new, or address a conflict.

Surface fears often appear in the form of actions. For instance, you may have a surface fear triggered by getting on an airplane. Surface fears can take the size and shape of just about anything given the right circumstances.

Deeply Rooted Fears

Deeply rooted fears are influenced by your inner state of mind, which reflects your self-efficacy (confidence in your abilities) and self-image. Your deeply rooted fears respond to how your ego processes things at the surface level. In simpler terms, the things you experience as a surface fear originate from a deeply rooted fear.

For example, my deeply rooted fear of judgment has contributed to my perfectionism which I experience every time I do creative work such as writing this book.

Deeply rooted fears rule your life. They guide your decisions and trickle into everything you do. The challenge of investigating your deeply ingrained fears is that they're buried deep within your subconscious mind. Like weeds, they can't be cut off at the surface to get rid of them. They take work to unearth. You need to dig them up and expose what lies at their roots. When you discover what's at the core of your fear, you can name it, and when you name your fear, you take back your power.

Please Note: Working through your deeply rooted fears may require more support than this book alone can offer. If it's available to you, I suggest tackling them with a licensed therapist or counselor.

Dig Up The Roots Of Your Fear

My best friend Brandy is an incredible hairstylist. She's excellent at color theory. Her colleagues often ask her to teach color education classes. Her answer is always no because Brandy is terrified of public speaking.

Curious about what's at the root of that fear, I asked her, "When it comes to public speaking, what are you really afraid of?" Her responses were what I'd expect from someone afraid of speaking in front of people.

* I'm afraid I will mispronounce a word, and people will laugh at me.
* I'm afraid someone will ask a question to which I don't know the answer.
* I'm afraid to have everyone's eyes on me and become the center of attention.

What she shared were her surface fears. Unsatisfied, I continued to dig.

Brandy shared that she's been teased in the past about the way she speaks. Recalling a specific incident during college where a friend declared that she was "too attractive to speak like that."

Bingo! I located a root. If I kept digging, I knew I could follow that root like a thread to other instances where someone made Brandy feel small based on her accent. It's no wonder she developed a fear of public speaking. I didn't push further.

To uncover what lies at the root of your fear, you must figure out what you're really afraid of. Let's start there.

What am I really afraid of?

The first step to uncovering the roots of your fear is asking yourself, "When it comes to (a thing that you're afraid to do), what am I really afraid of?" It's a straightforward question but the key is listening intentionally for the answers that surface. Make a list of every answer.

Once you have your list, it's time to dig deeper into why

you're afraid of those things. Go through your list and for every fear that you wrote down, ask yourself, "Why am I afraid of this thing?" Write down every thought that comes to mind.

Here are some additional questions that you can ask yourself to dig deeper:

* Am I afraid of feeling a feeling? Like embarrassed, ashamed, or overwhelmed.
* Am I trying to protect myself from a particular outcome? Like failure, rejection, judgment, or uncertainty.
* Does this situation spark negative memories? Are there connections between these experiences?

As you're going through this process, it is helpful to try to pinpoint specific memories. Can you recall an incident from your past when the thing that you fear actually happened? For example, was there a time that you mispronounced a word at work and people laughed?

It's unfortunate, but the moments when people make us feel unsafe, less than, or judged tend to stick out like sore thumbs. They're good indicators of where the roots of some of our deepest fears lie. Your deeply rooted fears are often reinforced unknowingly by others.

Try to trace the roots of your fear back as far as you can. Did you notice any patterns? Did certain experiences come up more than once?

Disprove The Stories About Yourself Created By Fear

We tell ourselves lots of stories. True stories. Slightly embellished stories. And stories about ourselves that are unkind.

We tend to use our fears as source material for the stories we tell ourselves.

"I don't have the type of body to wear a bikini." "I'm not smart enough to change careers." "I'm not loveable."

It is difficult for fear to sustain itself when you are able to dismiss the aspects of it that make it threatening. Disprove those stories by looking for evidence that they aren't true instead of piling on more evidence to confirm our fears. I call this showing your receipts.

What stories are you telling yourself? What meaning have you attached to them? Are the stories true?

Show Your Receipts

EXERCISE

What story about yourself has fear created? Is that story true? What evidence can you show to prove the story is false?

Amanda's Fear Fable

It was abandonment. Like, I can't even say the words right now. He just left.

We'd been together for seven years. Then, one day he just never came home. It was one of those situations where you're like, "Is this really happening?"

I didn't know what to do. I had so much to figure out, but I had a moment where I just knew this was not how my story ended. I had a choice: I could stay stuck in fear or push beyond it. I had nothing to lose cause there wasn't much left.

I let myself go crazy in a good way. Saying yes to things. I let spontaneity lead me. I put myself in social situations I would have never put myself in. I put myself in work situations where I would have played small. I put myself out there, and it was great.

Fast forward years later, after rebuilding my life, I didn't realize I was unconsciously making relationship choices and saying yes to things that I knew would not end well. Saying yes had become safe for me.

I thought I had moved past the fear that I had from the abandonment. I had done the work. But I realized I was afraid to connect with another person at that level again. I was overcompensating for my fears.

The biggest lesson learned through all that was that I had to be willing to seek a relationship even if I was afraid. Especially since that is something that I want in my life.

Amanda Shell

The Greatest Threats Come From Within Yourself

If you're not familiar with the boy wizard Harry Potter and his wizarding world, this reference to a "boggart" requires some explanation.

A bit of background: In *Harry Potter and the Prisoner of Azkaban* by J.K. Rowling, Professor Lupin introduces his Defense Against the Dark Arts class to a boggart in a wardrobe. Professor Lupin's students learn that a boggart is a shape-shifting creature that takes the "shape of whatever it thinks will frighten us most." Professor Lupin goes on to teach the class the charm and corresponding incantation to finish a boggart.

I get it; you're a muggle (non-magical person). Not a Potterhead. You have no clue what a boggart is. In muggle terms, a boggart is a shapeshifter that takes the shape of the observer's deepest fear. If your biggest fear is a fear of frogs, the boggart will appear to you as a frog.

The way to defeat a boggart is to cast the "Riddikulus" spell and force it to take an amusing shape instead of a scary one. Successful execution of this spell causes a boggart to be dispelled in laughter and amusement.

In the movie, the students line up individually to take their turn with the boggart. They conjure up a range of shapes for the boggart to assume, forcing it to shift from a giant black spider into a clumsy spider on roller skates. The students face their fears rather than cowering or running away.

This scene demonstrates an important lesson about understanding the Chorus of Fear: the greatest threat to our ability to show courage comes from within ourselves rather than outside.

Fear is stifling. It's disruptive. But there is something game-changing about realizing that the real threats to your ability to live an extraordinary life in full technicolor are born from your own heart. This makes you wonder, is the boggart scary, or is it simply a mirror? We can debate the answer to this question another time. I want to bring your attention back to your deeply-rooted fears.

Boggarts and deeply rooted fears have one thing in common. They are influenced by what's going on in your mind. If you probe further into your deeply rooted fears, you can trace them back to a single underlying fear.

It's the fear that you can't handle whatever happens next.

Hidden within every playlist created by the Chorus of Fear is a subliminal message saying, "I can't handle this."

I can't handle failure.

I can't handle getting rejected for the job.

I can't handle everything that comes with my success.

I can't handle my kids growing up.

I can't handle getting older.

I can't handle my parents dying.

Within all of that, there's an encouraging piece of truth. You have survived 100% of your worst days so far. This is proof enough that you can do hard things. You are a survivor. It doesn't matter what you've survived. Only that you survived. You can handle the things that life throws at you, even if you are afraid.

This truth underscores why I stated in Chapter 1, "Being fearless is not a prerequisite for living a big life." You don't have to learn to be fearless to stop your fear from having all the fun because knowing in your heart that you can handle anything that comes your way means you have nothing to fear.

So take action again and again. Keep going. You will accomplish great things if you face your fears head-on rather than being held back by them.

Dealing with your fears just comes down to having the courage to tell the Chorus of Fear, "Be quiet. I can handle this."

ADVICE #3

Key Takeaways

1. Acknowledging that you feel afraid is the first step that you can take toward silencing the Chorus of Fear. It's a simple yet overlooked step.

2. We experience fear at two levels: on the surface and deeply rooted within our minds. Surface fears are influenced by the situations we face every day. Our inner state of mind influences deeply rooted fears.

3. Pausing to ask yourself, "What am I really afraid of?" allows you to decide if you want to move forward intentionally.

4. We use fear to create stories about what we are capable of achieving. Show your receipts. Look to your past experiences as evidence that those stories aren't true.

SCIENCE
YES!

ADVICE #4:

Give More Energy To The Best-Case Scenario

While on a trip to Key West, my husband and I decided to take our son snorkeling for the first time. He was fourteen and very obsessed with sharks. The Florida Keys being home to the only living coral reefs in North America made the opportunity seem perfect. I found a snorkeling tour operator online and made a reservation.

As soon as we checked in and met our captain, I knew we were in for an experience. He immediately warned us that it was jellyfish season. Telling us, "There are going to be jellyfish. It could be three, or it could be 300. We won't know until we get out there. So you have to decide now, do you still want to go? Do you want to risk it?"

Oh. Hell. No.

This revelation made me pause. I hadn't planned to snorkel with jellyfish. My idea of snorkeling was some version of me finding Nemo and his friends swimming around the reef being cute.

I wanted zero parts of my body floating in the ocean with jellyfish swarming around.

But I'm a mom who encourages her child to "seek adventure" and "try new things." I suggested this trip. I didn't want to be the Debbie Downer.

I asked my son if he still wanted to go snorkeling. He said, "Yes."

So I'm like, "Ok. We're going for it."

After a short catamaran ride beneath the perfectly blue skies of the Florida Keys, we arrived at the coral reef. I started questioning the sanity of listening to a fourteen-year-old before we even dropped anchor. Peeking over the rail of the catamaran into the water, I spotted dinner plate-sized jellyfish lazily floating by. My thoughts immediately went into overdrive, cranking out the worst-case scenarios in vivid detail.

What's the worst that could happen? Um, a lot!

I could be stung by a jellyfish. That could be painful.

It's possible that I'm not as strong a swimmer as I believe myself to be. I haven't taken lessons since the 7th grade. I could drown.

It's probably not a good time to think about sharks.

I could be swept up in a jellyfish swarm and stung hundreds of times. Don't you remember what happened to Thomas from *My Girl* with those bees?

That scenario led me down a precariously slippery slope that started with the realization that I don't know if I'm allergic to jellyfish venom and ended with I don't have an epi-pen. What if I have a medical emergency while floating in the middle of the ocean?

To provide comfort and possibly avoid getting 1-star reviews on Google, Captain Morgan gave a pep talk. He told us that if we swam past the initial wall of jellyfish into the shallower waters, there'd be fewer jellyfish to deal with and a great view of the coral reef below.

I wanted that view, but was seeing the coral reef worth facing off with the jellyfish?

While listening to our captain's pep talk, I took a step back mentally to think through what was realistically the worst that could happen. A single outcome surfaced. I could be stung. That was the uncomfortable reality that the Chorus of Fear told me to avoid.

With that sense of clarity, I decided I would still snorkel the coral reef. Possibly getting stung by jellyfish was a risk I was willing to live with. Which meant there was only one thing left for me to do, I needed to get in the water.

Tentatively my husband and I made our way over to the catamaran's tiny ladder and swam away from the boat. Almost immediately, one of the tour guides in the water nearby asked us if we'd like to swim to the reef. He told us to follow him, and he would push the jellyfish out of the way. I'm not kidding when I tell you this guy was moving the jellyfish with his bare hands, and we swam over the top of them.

Having him sink the jellyfish was great, but I still had to look out for the ones he missed. Swimming behind him, I focused on maneuvering around and dodging rogue jellyfish. At some point, I remembered to look down. Imagine my surprise when I realized I was swimming over the reef and missing the view.

Be Careful Not To Miss The Reef

Even though I decided the risk of being stung was worth seeing the reef, I hadn't surrendered to the possibility that it might happen. I was giving all my precious energy to avoiding the worst-case scenario and nothing to enjoying the snorkel experience.

I didn't sign up to go snorkeling because I wanted to spend the entire time staring at the backside of my tour guide.

Do you get married to spend all of your energy focused on the possibility you might get a divorce?

Do you start a business to spend all of your energy focused on the chance you may fail?

Of course not! You do those things because there's something you desire to experience, learn or gain. The error of giving too much energy to think about the worst-case scenario is that you stay stuck there. You don't enjoy the experience. You don't recognize the lessons learned. You don't gain anything. You only see the next obstacle to avoid, never glancing around to catch the view. And you end up missing the reef.

For the record, I was stung twice. It wasn't that bad.

I learned that to give more energy to the best-case scenario, you must surrender to the possibility that you might not get what you imagined. The things you want for your life rarely arrive packaged neatly, sporting a big red bow. More often than not, they come bundled with challenges for you to overcome, but they can still turn out to be blessings.

Confront The Worst-Case Scenario

Before we used cell phone games to distract us while standing in the grocery store checkout line, flipping through the tabloids filled that void. Tabloid magazines relied on wild attention-grabbing headlines like "Bat Boy Captured by the FBI" or "Inside Tom Cruise's House of Horrors" to pique our interest. I want to believe that no one thinks those tabloid stories are true. Still, that has never stopped me from flipping through the pages while waiting to pay for my groceries.

While under the influence of the Chorus of Fear, our thoughts are like tabloid headlines explicitly designed to make us pay attention to them. Even in the face of those exaggerated claims, we choose to give a lot of energy and attention to stories we don't fully believe. We know logically they are twisted versions of a reality that hasn't happened, but we haven't taken a step back to consider a more balanced perspective. We let tabloid-style stories of the worst-case scenario dominate our decision-making. We call it catastrophizing (or catastrophic thinking).

Catastrophizing tends to focus on the worst possible outcomes of an event. We use catastrophizing as an emotional crutch to protect ourselves in uncertain situations, imagining the worst possible scenarios so that we won't be caught off guard if they happen.

The simplest way to counteract catastrophizing is to get specific about what is most likely the worst-case scenario. Doing this saps it of much of its anxiety-inducing power. When you're clear on what could realistically happen, you're less likely to participate in a catastrophic level of irrational thinking, making the situation feel less scary. Then, you can step back and look objectively at what could happen and decide on your next steps.

I want you to stop romanticizing the worst-case scenario and approach it with a hefty dose of realism. Here's how to confront the worst-case scenario:

STEP 1. MAKE A LIST OF THE WORST-CASE SCENARIOS.

Ask yourself, "What am I afraid might happen if I (insert thing you're afraid to do)?"

The Chorus of Fear is a great illusionist. It is skilled at playing up excuses, distorting the truth, and warping reality. Often the outcomes you experience are not as bad as the Chorus of Fear has convinced you they will be, but you won't realize that until you think logically.

Pause. Breathe deeply to clear your mind. Then, take a moment to think about all of the fears you are feeling. Write them down. Jot down any thoughts or anxieties that pop up.

Feel your feelings. Remember that is a part of acknowledging your fear. Don't try to minimize or judge the ideas that bubble up to the surface. Just dump all of your irrational thoughts onto the paper.

It is your opportunity to confront the worst-case scenarios that you are entertaining. Gather them together and shine a light on them.

STEP 2. ASK YOURSELF, "IS THIS REALISTIC OR EVEN POSSIBLE?"

Ask yourself for each fear you wrote down: "Is this fear realistic or even possible?"

We often get hung up on vague fears without considering whether or not they're possible. Stop fixating on your worries. Fact check them to see if they're true.

Is this fear realistic? Is it possible for it to happen?

Realizing a specific fear isn't likely to happen can make it go away.

When I was weighing the decision of whether or not to go snorkeling, one of my fears was the possibility that I was allergic to jellyfish venom. It could be a real fear for someone else, but that wasn't the case for me. I've visited the beaches of Florida my entire life, and I was sure I'd been stung by jellyfish before. I'd been stung by a bee, and I was fine. I used that reasoning to conclude that I wasn't allergic to jellyfish venom.

STEP 3. ASK YOURSELF, "IF THE WORST-CASE SCENARIO DID HAPPEN, WHAT WOULD THE CONSEQUENCES BE?"

For the fears that remain after the previous step, ask yourself, "If the worst-case scenario did happen, what would the consequences be?"

Write down what you fear are the consequences of moving forward.

I'm a realist. I'd rather you give me the truth straight, so I can prepare myself to deal with it. I'm not into selling you the idea that this will be unicorns and rainbows all the time (probably not even most of the time).

Being realistic is a big part of silencing the Chorus of Fear. It's ok to consider the consequences. To make the best decision possible, you need a clear understanding of the risks and what is at stake to lose. Doing this helps you calculate the risk versus the reward.

STEP 4. MAKE A LIST OF ALL THE WONDERFUL THINGS THAT COULD HAPPEN.

Ask yourself, "What is the best that could happen?"

It's a tragedy that the default setting of our minds is to create a variety of negative outcomes almost effortlessly. Imagine how powerful you would be if your mind defaulted to creating an abundance of favorable results in response to uncertainty. It would be an amazing superpower.

Until then, make a list of all the wonderful things that could happen. Write down every positive thought, feeling, and outcome you can dream up.

Some wonderful things to consider:

* How will you feel after you finish? Proud? Strong? Joyous?
* What if everything worked out better than you thought? What would that look like?
* What opportunities could this lead to? What doors could be open?
* What is the best that could happen if the worst thing happened?

Stretch yourself to create a good list. If the Chorus of Fear provided you with five reasons why you shouldn't do it, try to think of six reasons why it would be awesome. You can get imaginative, dreaming up all the wonderful things that could happen. So let your mind linger here a bit longer.

STEP 5. MAKE A DECISION.

Once you've run both scenarios, you must decide. You're crystal clear on what's the worst that could realistically happen. You know what the consequences could be. But you're also armed with a list of wonderful outcomes. Which are you willing to live with?

I won't assume you will keep going once you reach this step. It is your decision. Review everything you've written. Are you willing to accept the potential consequences, good or bad? Is it worth the risk?

Make your decision. Then, move forward with confidence.

If you're still unsure, I made a decision tree to help you decide.

Should I Take This Risk

Should I take this risk?

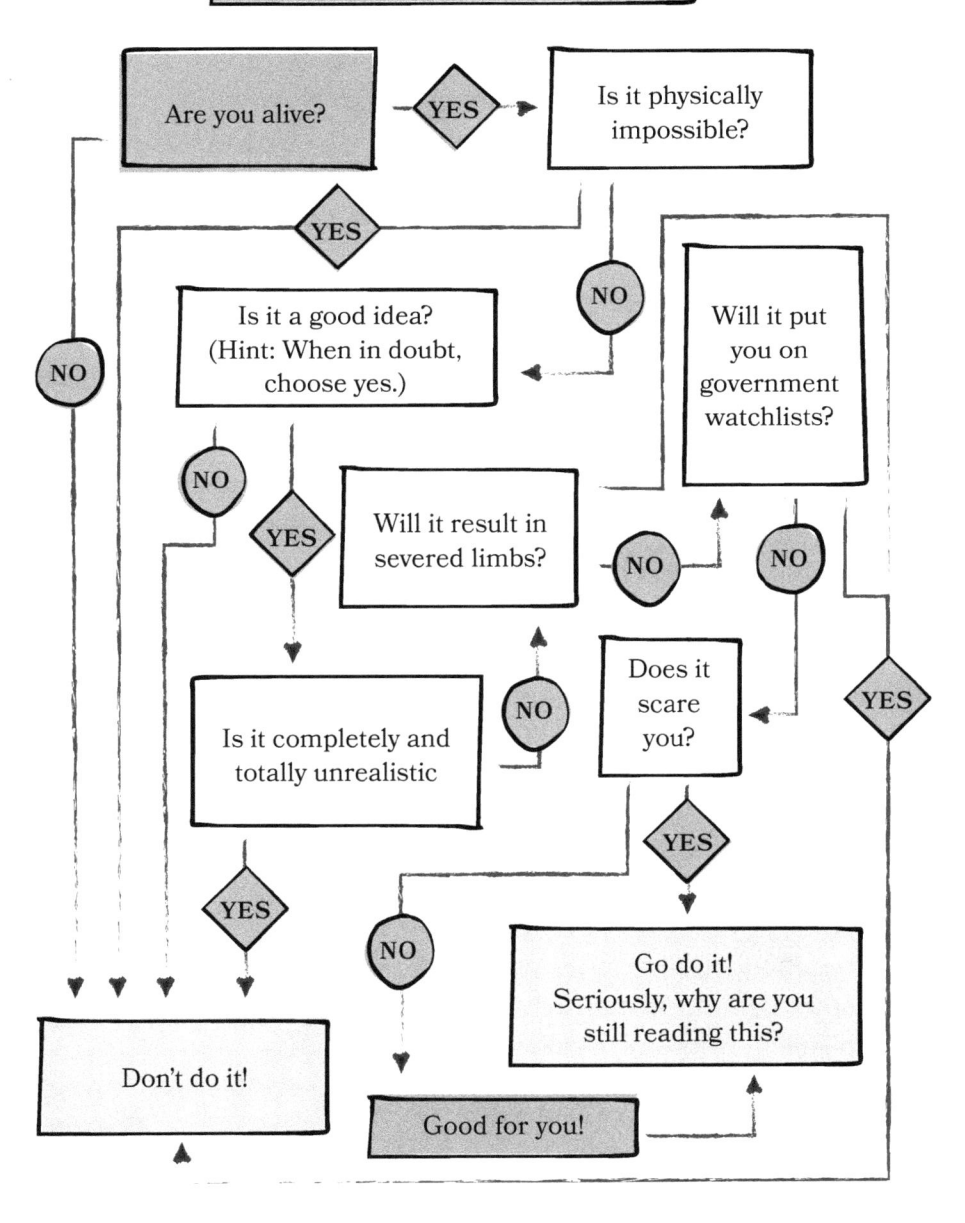

- **Are you alive?** → NO → Don't do it!
- **Are you alive?** → YES → **Is it physically impossible?**
  - YES → Don't do it!
  - NO → **Is it a good idea?** (Hint: When in doubt, choose yes.)
    - NO → Don't do it!
    - YES → **Will it result in severed limbs?**
      - YES → **Is it completely and totally unrealistic**
        - YES → Don't do it!
        - NO → Good for you!
      - NO → **Does it scare you?**
        - NO → **Will it put you on government watchlists?**
          - NO → Good for you!
          - YES → Go do it! Seriously, why are you still reading this?
        - YES → Go do it! Seriously, why are you still reading this?

Christa's Fear Fable

I started traveling because there's a big world out there, and I wanted to see it. I was in my twenties. I decided to go on a solo trip even though none of my family had left the United States of America. I went to Puerto Rico. I know it's a part of the United States, but in my mind, it was still foreign enough. I thought I was going to get lost. My Spanish is not that great. I decided to go anyway. I did it by myself.

Yes, I was scared, but I was like, "The worst that could happen is... Actually, I don't want to think about the worst that can happen." I had to lean into this idea that there are kind people in the world. The thing that got me through that experience, quite frankly, was Facebook. I shared minute-by-minute details about my trip as status updates. Like "just landed," "got to my hotel," or "I'm at the beach."

At that moment, I was scared. I wasn't sure how I was going to move about. I just clicked right into myself. It turned out to be a great experience and opened me up to becoming a solo traveler.

It has been 20 years, and I still mostly travel alone. Every time I go on a solo trip, I have this tiny bit of fear. I'm like, "Oh my God, it's a new place. Am I going to get lost? Am I going to get hurt?" There have been trips that I've taken since then where I've thought, "I'm gonna die today because I got in some crazy accident." But that hasn't stopped me from thinking about and planning where I'm going next.

Christa David

Stop Treating Your Decisions Like Amusement Park Rides

I have a theory.

There are two types of people: those who love roller coasters and those who hate them. There isn't a middle ground. I suspect this is because the decision to ride a roller coaster is a firm commitment.

Picture it.

You wait in the queue. Once it's your turn, you walk over and get in the seat. You pull the harness down over your head. An attendant comes by to check that your harness is secure. You're strapped into the seat, waiting for the ride to start. The attendant gives the all-clear signal, and the train moves forward on the track.

Freeze frame.

Until that point, you could have changed your mind and backed out of riding the roller coaster. Now that the train is in motion, it's too late to change your mind. You can't stop the rollercoaster. You're at the mercy of the experience until it is over. There is no off-ramp to steer the train towards to let you off the ride.

Most people treat decision-making like riding roller coasters. They make a decision and believe they have to see that decision through until the end, even if what once felt like a thrilling decision now has them screaming in pure terror. Life is not an amusement park ride, there are off ramps, and you can use them to get off the ride.

Very few decisions that, once made, can't be unmade. Off ramps are your way out of a decision that you made. You can change your course despite what you've been taught to believe.

I think of off ramps as UNO "Reverse" cards for your decisions. Has life been throwing out too many draw-four cards lately? No problem. Throw out your "Reverse" card and change direction.

For example, let's say you've decided to dip your toe into the wild world of online dating. After a few weird dates, you decide it isn't for you and deactivate your dating profiles. That's you utilizing your off-ramp. You tried it but didn't love it, so you deactivated it. You're not obligated to stick to that decision for a set amount of time. You can get off the ride as soon as you realize it's no longer fun.

The cool thing about off-ramps is that you can decide to be bold and move forward with the location of the closest off-ramp tucked in your back pocket just in case things start to go sideways. Take Christa's story as an example. She could have purchased trip cancellation insurance to use as an off-ramp. That way, she'd have the security of knowing that if she changed her mind and decided not to go to Puerto Rico, she could cancel her trip with minimal penalties.

On the flip side, you can make a decision believing you don't need an off-ramp only to realize that you need to find one immediately. It happens, and it's nothing to be ashamed of. Sometimes despite your best efforts and carefully calculated decisions, things do not go as planned. If you don't have an off-ramp readily available, you can start looking for one as soon as you know you need it.

You'll rarely encounter an opportunity that genuinely has no off ramps. I won't say it never happens because anything is possible. You're more likely to find yourself in a situation where the off-ramp isn't apparent or immediately available. If that happens, I believe how you deal with that situation can be found in the experience of riding a roller coaster.

While strapped in the seat, butterflies dance in your stomach as the train climbs the steep incline. You brace yourself as you anticipate feeling the first big drop in your stomach. Your body is tense, your knuckles are white, and suddenly you are sailing down the track. It's scary. After a few seconds, you realize you are handling it. You are riding the rollercoaster. Soon enough, the ride is over. You get off shaken but not stirred.

Everything in life is impermanent. Nothing can or will last forever. Keep looking for your off-ramps. And when you need one, feel free to use it.

Find Your Off-Ramps

EXERCISE

A decision is just a decision, and you can make another decision. Off-ramps are your way out of a decision you've made. You can identify them before you decide to move forward. Or you can figure them out once the decision is made. Use the space to write out one or two possible off-ramp ideas.

_____
_____
_____
_____
_____
_____
_____
_____
_____
_____
_____
_____
_____
_____
_____
_____

Andria's Fear Fable

I was an undergrad in college, taking several introductory classes. I planned to be a business major. During that time, I took two classes that changed my life and my mind about what I thought I was in college for. One was humanistic tradition, which is a cross between philosophy and history. It was a class where I walked in thinking I knew what I believed, but I left every class thinking, "I don't know what I believe anymore. " The other class was sociology. I fell in love with personal development. I wanted to learn everything there was about it. I started toying with the idea of switching majors.

Many questions popped into my brain, like, "What do you do with a sociology degree? How do you make money learning about philosophy? What philosopher do you know out there thriving?"

It went against the reason why I was in college. I was the first person in my family to go to college. I was there to make something of myself and escape the web of poverty that I was born into. So I continued with my business degree.

Fast forward some years, I have a six-month-old daughter and I'm back in school to get my MBA. One semester into my MBA program, I learned there was another program where I could get an MBA with a concentration in organizational behavior. I took one course called organizational management behavior. It was the same stuff that I fell in love with during undergrad.

I asked my advisor if I could switch my concentration. That's when I found out the organizational behavior track is taught in a cohort, and I'd have to wait until next Fall to start. I wouldn't be done for another year and a half if I switched.

This time I was committed to switching but wasn't committed to getting off schedule. So I finished another business degree. I made a decision that did not make me happy but made me feel safe. Every time I think about it, there's a tinge of regret. I always wonder where I would be if I had followed those gut feelings.

Andria Giles

ADVICE #4

Key Takeaways

1. Focusing on the worst-case scenario leads to catastrophizing. When you're clear on the worst-case scenario, you're less likely to participate in that level of irrational thinking.

2. Give just as much energy, if not more, to imagining the best possible outcomes. Ask yourself, "What is the best that can happen?" Allow your imagination to fill in the gaps with all the wonderful things.

3. Decide which outcomes you can live with. Then, make a decision.

4. Don't treat your decisions like riding a roller coaster. You can change your mind. Look for the off-ramps and use them.

82

ADVICE #5:

Take Tiny Action To Build Your Courage

I have my husband to thank for my first business. I didn't realize it then, but he planted the seed that eventually grew into my t-shirt line Antisparkle Apparel. I remember the exact moment that it happened. We were in the craft store one afternoon during Spring break. I was teaching at the time. We were browsing the aisles and at the end of one was a display for a personal screen printing machine. My husband casually suggested that I buy it and start making t-shirts. I thought he was crazy. I actually said, "That's crazy," out loud. I didn't consider it much; I bought my craft supplies, and we left.

That's the thing about planting seeds; if you water them, they begin to grow. I kept thinking about that screen printing machine after we got home. I loved wearing cool t-shirts. The realization that I could learn to design my own t-shirts and that my husband had encouraged me to spend several hundred dollars on a screen printing machine made me believe I could do it. I returned to the craft store a few days later and bought that screen printing machine. Three weeks later, I started an Etsy shop to sell my t-shirts.

I had no experience with screen printing. I didn't know how to use design software. I couldn't draw. But there I was, starting a very visual and graphics-focused business. I wasn't even a little ready, but I started anyway.

It was an ugly start. That didn't matter. People bought my t-shirts anyway.

The best time to start pursuing your goals, dreams, and desires is before you're ready. You'll never feel prepared enough. Things will not be perfect. You might not feel like it's the best you can do, but it'll be good enough to start.

You won't regret taking those first steps. When you're just starting, optimism and enthusiasm are on your side. Sort of like beginner's luck. They provide you with the initial boost that propels you forward. And if you want it, that will be enough to help you keep going until you find your footing.

Start Before You're Ready. Do It Afraid.

This is for the planners, the overthinkers, and the people who need every step laid out in precise detail before they even consider making a move. Listen up!

When taking action, start before you're ready and do it afraid.

It can be tempting to hide behind a self-imposed barrier of waiting for the "perfect time" or until you "feel ready."

You'll never be totally ready. The timing may never be right. And the Chorus of Fear will slip in to sing its seductive siren song.

It isn't a knock against you or your abilities. I believe you are perfectly capable. But readiness isn't something you switch on at will like a lamp. It doesn't rush out, book a red-eye flight, and show up in the morning just because you called. Readiness is earned. You earn it piece by piece. Very often at the cost of dancing to the

Chorus of Fear's greatest hits album of anxiety, self-doubt, and uncertainty. Readiness comes with taking action. You have to do the work to feel ready. You have to be a little bold.

As the famous proverb states, "Fortune favors the bold," but I'd like to amend it to point out that so does opportunity.

The dictionary defines opportunity as "a set of circumstances that makes it possible to do something." So it isn't a stretch to say that opportunity unlocks the door that leads to possibility. What I find interesting is that you can't plan for an opportunity. There are many instances in life where an opportunity shows up, shining, enticing, and willing you to take it. You must take the opportunity even if you don't feel ready. You have to have faith in yourself. You have to trust and believe that you will handle whatever happens.

Opportunity, just like time, does not care that you are not currently feeling ready enough to start. It will pass you by to find someone who feels bold enough to put their comfort and ego on the line. And that's the real issue at the heart of this, isn't it?

To seize an opportunity, you must be willing to disrupt your carefully crafted illusion of comfort and expose your sensitive ego to the possibility of disappointment. You cannot accept an opportunity without accepting some amount of risk. Waiting until you're ready may cause you to miss significant opportunities like promotions or a shot at love.

Delaying action makes those uncomfortable feelings stronger. Putting it off for another time or waiting for the next opportunity only makes it much harder to start. For instance, waiting until the cards line up, the bank account is where you think it needs to be, or the people in your life feel the same way doesn't make it easier to get started a month from now. It's not going to be any easier tomorrow. The opposite happens. Delaying allows the Chorus of Fear to get stronger. Giving it extra time to string together an even better chart-topping playlist to sing you out of trying. I'll repeat it, start today. Do it afraid.

XayLi's Fear Fable

I was born in Trinidad, moved to New York around sixteen, and lived there for twelve years. I always felt the itch to leave. New York is amazing, but I got to a point where I realized that I wasn't living. I had become a shell of a person.

My realization came when I noticed it's only warm for three months out of the year. I used to get so excited for those few months. Then, there would be nine months of dark, cold weather. So the weather, dealing with depression, anxiety, and running my own business made New York City feel too much.

The only thing that kept me there was my partner. He was born and bred in Brooklyn. He wasn't leaving. Our family was there. Everyone and everything that we knew was in New York.

When we went through a period of separation, I knew it was my chance to leave and create roots somewhere else. I started looking for apartments in Dallas. I worked with a realtor. Once they found an apartment for me, I locked myself into a 16-month lease. I did that intentionally so no one could talk me out of moving. Then, I told my mom, dad, and ex-partner that I was leaving.

During the time between telling everyone and boarding the plane, I kept asking myself, "What the heck are you doing?" I'd never been to Dallas. I'd never been to Texas. I'd never been far away from New York. All I knew was that a beautiful apartment was waiting for me on the other side.

I'm still here four years later. My partner lives in Dallas now. I wouldn't be here on this side if I had not pushed through that fear. Moving to Dallas completely changed my life in the most significant way ever.

XayLi Barclay

Remember, my goal with this book isn't to teach you to be fearless. It is to help you make bold moves even if you're afraid. I want you to act courageously instead of fearless because courage is taking action despite your fear.

Eddie Rickenbacker stated this so eloquently when he said, "Courage is doing what you're afraid to do. There can be no courage unless you're scared."

If you wait until you feel brave, you will be waiting forever. Aiming to be fearless is an impossible standard to meet. It's just not how we humans are built. Plus, no rule says you must wait until you have enough courage to start. Realistically, how would you measure that? What amount of courage is enough? It's not like you can go into your pantry, grab a bag of courage and scoop it out by the cup like you do flour. "Let's see, this recipe for alligator wrestling requires five cups of courage." That's not how this works. If it did, I would have sold you a bag of courage, not a book.

You don't need to make giant leaps or have unlimited courage to start. You can achieve the same results by taking tiny action and building your courage in small doses. It's the best way to make those bold moves even if the Chorus of Fear has just queued up an encore performance to rival Mariah Carey at Christmas time.

Practice Taking Tiny Action

Does the thought of starting make you feel overwhelmed? If so, congratulations! It makes you normal.

Sometimes we want to accomplish something and be bold, and that thing still feels too far out of reach. Somehow the work needed to make that thing happen is not only overwhelming to take on but also a bit elusive. Whenever I feel hesitant about getting started and taking action, it's because I'm thinking about the big picture, and I feel intimidated by it.

Dream big. Reach for the stars. The sky is not the limit.

These are all things that the well-meaning people in our lives have said to us to get us to go after what we want. I'm even guilty of saying similar things to my clients. I love thinking about the big picture. There are benefits to letting your imagination dream as big as it dares. While this is an excellent practice for setting goals and planning your moves, it's less useful once it's time to take action. Using the big picture as your focal point as you work up the nerve to get started is a recipe for overwhelm. Instead of focusing on the big picture, I want to offer you a better way to take action in your life—practice taking tiny action.

A tiny action is a bite-sized action step. Taking tiny action is breaking your action steps into smaller, less energy-consuming, and less overwhelming steps.

For example, practicing tiny action is reading for 10 minutes a day to expand your way of thinking. Sending one query a day to find an agent to represent your book. Washing, folding, and putting away a load of laundry every day versus letting it pile up for the weekend. Breaking those large action steps down into something that feels manageable shifts you from that place of fear, analysis paralysis, and overwhelm.

Taking tiny action creates less resistance.

Every action you take requires a certain amount of effort to start. In Chemistry, this is called activation energy, which refers to the minimum energy needed for a reaction. (Yay! Science!) Outside the lab, you can apply the idea behind activation energy to your life.

You've probably realized getting started is often the most challenging part of taking action. That's because the activation energy required to begin the process is high.

For instance, dragging yourself off of the couch and away from your latest Netflix binge to go to the gym requires more activation energy than getting up to do 10 minutes of yoga in your living room. Just like spending countless hours stressing and talking about sending an email requires more energy than actually sending the email.

If the activation energy needed to do something is too high, you will most likely not do the action. Simply put, tiny actions require less effort and energy. They are easier to do.

I'm not a runner. In high school, I vividly remember my physical education teacher freshman year yelling at a group of friends and me as we casually strolled around the track during our physical fitness test. We were supposed to be running a mile.

See? Not a runner. Still, I'd always wondered if I had the mental toughness to complete a half marathon. So I signed up for one. I won't lie. I did not finish my half marathon training. There are several reasons, but the most important one is that I realized as I was training that I don't enjoy running. It didn't deter me. I still wanted to cross "complete a half marathon" off of my bucket list.

One crisp morning in November, I got up at the butt crack of dawn to queue up with thousands of people for the Space Coast Half Marathon. My husband and friend were faster than me, so I had to run it alone.

I was about four miles in when the Chorus of Fear showed up with an unhelpful playlist titled "It's not too late to turn around." It was also around this time that the fastest female runner lapped me.

I've always wondered how anyone could convince themselves to go out and run 13 miles. Now I know. It turns out that marathons are completed one step at a time. In my case, I did it by jogging to the next house, a random spot in the distance, or the refreshment station. (The refreshment stations and people handing out free chocolate along the route were the real marathon MVPs.) I mentally broke the race course into small actions instead of focusing on how much I had left to go.

As I continued to walk and jog along, I felt an internal push to keep going. After a while, it no longer made sense to turn around because it would have taken the same amount of effort to finish. And by then, I was confident I would reach the finish line.

I learned many lessons during that marathon, but the one that sticks with me is how taking tiny actions increases your confidence, leading to more action-taking. There were moments when I doubted my ability to finish, but with each mile crossed, my confidence soared. I wanted to keep going and receive my finishers medal. As you take action in small ways, your identity shifts, and you begin to see yourself as more capable and confident. You start to see yourself as an action taker. A person who gets stuff done. A person who completes half marathons. And now I don't run anymore, but I have this story that keeps me going.

After a while, those tiny actions begin to give way to something else—momentum. Momentum is such an interesting phenomenon because it becomes self-perpetuating at a certain point. You've probably experienced this while roller skating. The first few pushes forwards give your legs a workout, but as you pick up speed and build momentum, the rollerskates continue to glide along without additional pushes.

Tiny action seems insignificant at first, but over time that action compounds and delivers big results. Baby steps eventually turn into adult steps. Never underestimate the big importance of taking tiny action.

Break The Big Action Into Tiny Actions

EXERCISE

Everything in life that seems impossibly large is accomplished by taking tiny action steps. You don't need to do everything all at once. Break that significant action into something smaller and more manageable. Set a timer for 7 - 10 minutes. Then, use this space to brainstorm or mind map a list of small actions that will move you closer to what you're trying to achieve. Put a star next to your first tiny action.

Build Courage In Small Doses

As a creator, I've done plenty of scary things throughout my creative journey— selling at craft shows, pitching myself to the press, speaking in front of large groups, and manufacturing a product overseas, all through email. I have years of "taking the leap and building the parachute on the way down" type of experiences to pull from, but if I had to choose the single scariest thing I've done in my business so far, it would be launching a Kickstarter campaign.

Two years.

That's how long it took me to work up the courage to run a Kickstarter campaign for my planner, the Visionary Journal. I remember it so well.

Until that point, I had bootstrapped the entire design, creation, and production of the Visionary Journal. Buying supplies, hand making the original copies, and Google searching manufacturers until my eyes crossed. I had a clear vision of the look and feel of the planner I wanted to create and was determined to bring that exact vision to life. The problem? Producing a physical planner comes with lots of costs. I needed a way to get the necessary funding.

After many expensive mistakes (like paying for a production run of planners on my credit card), I finally decided to put my big girl panties on and create a Kickstarter campaign.

Kickstarter is a crowdfunding platform for creative projects. You set a funding goal, and people pledge money towards your project in exchange for rewards (usually early access to whatever you're creating). It sounds simple enough.

Well, there's a catch. It's all-or-nothing funding. It means your project has to meet or exceed its funding goal within 30 days, or you forfeit all of your pledges. Talk about pressure. I'm sweating just thinking about it.

The thought of putting so much hard work into building a campaign only to have it fail terrified me. The Chorus of Fear had a wonderful time developing a new playlist. What would people say about my business if I couldn't raise the funding? How would I come back after such a public failure? And don't get me started on my feelings about asking people for money.

Money is such a loaded topic. It's weird and uncomfortable. In the past, I've shied away from money conversations because they can be such a wild card. But to run a successful Kickstarter campaign, I would have to convince people that my idea was worth backing AND ask them to pledge their hard-earned dollars.

With the Chorus of Fear producing so many excuses and reasons not to launch the Kickstarter campaign, it's a wonder that I was able to pull it off. A few days before the start of my campaign, I had a game-changing shift in my perspective about what it means to show courage. I realized that having courage is not all or nothing.

My friend Manya once expertly explained, "We think we must summon the courage for the entire experience simultaneously. When sitting in front of an experience, we imagine the totality of courage needed. It will take two units of courage here, three there, four there, and five there. Suddenly you're up to 100 units of courage! And you're not sure if you can muster 100 units of courage right then. That can feel overwhelming, but you don't have to muster all the courage at once. You just have to muster the courage for the next thing. So I just break it down into the smallest unit where it doesn't feel like it requires a great deal of courage."

Courage is built in small doses. You can build up just enough courage to type up that email to your boss requesting a meeting to discuss your raise. Then, you can work up the courage to hit send. You can build up just enough courage to make an appointment with the dentist. Then, on the day of your appointment, you gather enough courage to get in the car and eventually sit in the dentist's chair.

I call this practicing micro courage. Micro courage is teaching yourself to be brave by taking tiny action steps.

Most people believe courage is something you're born with. And while there may be some people who are naturally braver than others, most of us have to learn and build courage over a lifetime. Courage is a skill; to get good at it, you must practice. Intentionally practicing acts of micro courage helps you become more comfortable with being uncomfortable.

Manya's Fear Fable

I wanted to be a person who skydives. I wanted to feel the freedom of it. I wanted a unique experience of seeing the world from that perspective. That's what I wanted to get out of it.

Was it scary to put on the harness? No. Was it scary to approach an airplane? No. Was it scary to get into an airplane? Not for me. I love airplanes.

So then you're going up into the sky. You're moving down the bench, waiting for your turn. Really at the end of the day, jumping out of an airplane for me was leaning back into the guy who was tandem jumping with me. He leaned forward and pushed us out of the plane. And so it was, can I find the courage to lean back?

Manya Andrews Dotson

Getting back to my Kickstarter campaign, the biggest obstacle I faced was being brave enough to ask everyone I knew to support me. I didn't want to ask for the money even though I needed it. So I devised a plan that required only small doses of courage and made asking easy.

Here's how I practiced micro courage during my Kickstarter campaign:

I downloaded a list of all my friends on Facebook and put it into a spreadsheet. There were over 300+! I wrote a simple message about my campaign, including a video link, and asked for support. Every day of the campaign, I aimed to send that message to at least ten people from my spreadsheet.

To build my courage even faster, I ensured the first 100 people were mainly family and good friends. People I felt had the highest likelihood of saying "Yes." I wanted to get as many small wins as quickly as possible. Those initial supporters backing my project helped show me that my project was viable. Their excitement and support helped me keep asking until I reached my goal. When my campaign ended, I gained over $15k in funding, exceeding my goal.

You don't need to feel 100% ready to make a bold move. You don't need massive amounts of courage to achieve your goals. Starting small is enough. Launching and running a successful Kickstarter campaign taught me that micro courage is accepting that if you want to do something, you might feel uncomfortable doing it. Still, you go ahead and do it anyway.

How To Take Action When You Don't Know How Or Where To Start

We are rolling now. You feel fired up and ready to take tiny action. Your micro courage muscles can't wait to flex. You just have one last question: "How do I take action if I don't know where to start?"

I was anticipating this question. It always comes up. Sometimes you aren't sure where to start. I get it.

My no-fluff answer is you start by finding your step one.

Here's where it gets tricky. I can't tell you what your step one should be. Step one is different for everyone because it is determined by factors like your level of ambition, skills, resources, and the information you already have. It will take some effort on your part. You still have to get started, and your best shot at success is to start on step one.

Most people overthink starting. They make it way too complicated. Don't be like most people. The path of least resistance when getting started is to start with where you are and what you have available. The problem? Everyone thinks they need to know how to complete step ten when they haven't started on step one.

For instance, if you wanted to change careers, what would be step one? I couldn't give you an answer without asking for more information, but I can tell you what step one is not. Step one is not obsessing over job listings and becoming frustrated that you don't meet all the qualifications for the position you want to move into. It's also not submitting your resignation letter (not yet, at least).

Step one could be researching ways to fill the gaps in your qualifications. Maybe there's a certification program that you could enroll in. It could be scheduling time with your director at work or a career coach to discuss your possible career path. It could even be doing a cost and benefit analysis comparing your current role to the one you would like to move into.

Want to learn how to swim, but you've never set foot in a body of water? Step one is not registering for a triathlon three weeks from now. Step one might be going to Target to purchase a swimsuit and goggles. A better first step would be to join your local recreation center and sign up for swimming lessons.

Step one is a tiny action. Something that helps get you going but doesn't take up a lot of time or require a lot of energy. It's enough of an action that you can walk away satisfied with a quick win tucked into your back pocket while also shining a light on the path to step two.

Going back to my swimming example, if you registered for a triathlon three weeks from now as your step one, what would be your step two? You would need to complete that triathlon, but you would have skipped many steps. When would you learn to swim? When would you train? You create a situation for yourself where it's highly likely that you will fail. While I think failure can offer us some valuable insights, that's the opposite of what I want for you.

I can give you steps, but this is where those steps end. There is no five-step process for how to take action when you don't know how to start. It is assessing where you are in the process and what resources you have access to. Then, you find your step one and take the first step forward.

Clarity, progress, and all that other good stuff come from doing the work. No linear process or list of hacks will get you there. You have to do the work. The more that you move forward, the more information you receive. When you take action, you open up possibilities. Some paths will open to you that were unavailable before you started.

Find Your Step One

EXERCISE

Getting started often is the hardest part. Without a clearly defined path, it can be difficult to know where to start. The simplest way to get started is to find your step one and let the path unfold. Answer the following questions to discover your step one.

What are you trying to achieve?

_____
_____
_____
_____
_____
_____
_____
_____
_____
_____
_____
_____
_____
_____
_____
_____
_____
_____

What is the best and next logical step that you can take toward achieving your goal?

___

Is this a tiny action?	**YES / NO**
Is this the path of least resistance?	**YES / NO**
Will completing this step give you a quick win?	**YES / NO**
Does it shine a light on the path to step two?	**YES / NO**

If you answered yes to all four questions, you've found your step one. Congratulations!

If you answered no to any of the questions, revisit it to figure out how to get to step one.

Taking action when you feel uncertain is challenging because you want to get it right. So I wanted to offer a few more pieces of advice that you might find useful:

Permit yourself to take imperfect action. As writers, we use a concept called an SFD or "shitty first draft" to help us make progress. The idea is to get the words out and on paper, even if they're terrible. To complete your shitty first draft, you must permit yourself to write imperfectly. To put down words that aren't quite right. The same idea applies to taking action. You can still reach your destination even if your execution isn't as precise as Simone Biles competing in the floor exercise. Give yourself permission to mess it up because it will be messy.

Zoom in on your next step. Worrying about tomorrow is the thing that gets in the way of your ability to take action today. Wasting time ruminating over all the "what-if" questions about situations that haven't come to pass yet. Stop borrowing trouble from the future. Focus on the task at hand. Zoom in on your next step. You must dial in so that everything else is out of focus.

Keep taking action as long as it isn't to your detriment. seek safety and comfort, so taking action is not our defau׳ ting. Ironically, every dream, goal, and result achieved from taking action. It might be uncomfortable and pai keep taking action as long as it isn't causing irreversi׳ age. Discomfort is a side effect of taking action. You v you're doing it right because the thing you're tryinς requires action. Growth and comfort can't inhak space.

To sum it all up, what you are looking for is jι side of the act of doing. You have to commit to ta if it's not pretty.

Finally, after reading those tips, if you're still looking for a starting point, here are some tiny courage-building actions you can take today:

* Pick one thing that's been sitting on your to-do list for over a week. Set a timer for 30 minutes and see if you can finish it.
* Compliment a stranger. Does the woman on the train have cute shoes? Tell her. It gets you out of your comfort zone, makes you more assertive, and makes someone's day - win/win.
* Try a food that you've never tried before. You never know—it could be your new favorite meal.
* Engage in an experience that exposes you to something outside your usual leisure activities. Consider visiting a museum, volunteering at your local food pantry, or taking a floral arranging class.
* Ask someone out on a date. It is a bold move that will flex your blossoming courage muscles.
* Sign up for a new class at the gym. You'll feel a sense of accomplishment once you finish.
* [Do a] typically partnered activity alone. It helps you [learn to] enjoy your own company.
* [Try read]ing a book from a genre outside of your [choi]ces. You may discover a new interest.
* [Spend m]inutes expanding your mind beyond [w]hat you currently believe is possible
* [Dream a] bigger dream for yourself. Journal

[These] actions likely won't help you com[plete... they] will give you more and more cour[age...bi]t. Courage isn't finite. The more [you use it] it replenishes simply by doing

ADVICE #5

Key Takeaways

1. Start before you're ready. You'll never get started if you're waiting around to feel ready. Readiness is earned by taking action.

2. Practice taking tiny action. Break your goals or projects into smaller, less energy-consuming steps.

3. Courage isn't all or nothing. Build courage in small doses by practicing micro courage.

4. If you don't know where or how to start, focus on finding your step one. Step one is the path of least resistance and the next logical step.

104

ADVICE #6:

Celebrate Your Entire Journey

What would you do for a Klondike Bar?

As an 80s-baby and 90s-kid, it probably doesn't shock you that I spent a lot of time watching TV. Probably too much time. During the 90s, Nickelodeon was at its prime with TV shows and cartoons. Being a kid-focused network, they showed lots of commercials. Because of this, the jingle of the Klondike Bar ice cream commercials will forever live rent-free in my head.

"What would you doo-oo for a Klondike Bar?" Queue man barking like his dog to get rewarded with that chocolate-covered square of ice cream.

Here's my confession, I wouldn't do anything for a Klondike Bar. Not. One. Single. Thing. I never got the appeal. Plus, they were difficult to eat. The chocolate coating cracked under your fingers while the ice cream melted and ran down your hands. You were better off eating an ice cream bar; at least the cool ones had cartoon faces and bubblegum eyes. (90s kids, do you remember the Ninja Turtles ice cream bar?) Those Klondike Bar commercials never made sense to me. I didn't believe anyone would do anything for a Klondike Bar. At least no one that I knew. (By the way, I have the same feelings about York Peppermint Patties. I'm getting off track with my story.)

Now, if you want to talk about tasty treats, I'd be willing to do something strange; I'd like to direct your attention to Cheetos Puffs. Neon orange puffs of cheesy deliciousness. Yum! I would be willing to brave the poison ivy-filled forest and hike a portion of the Appalachian Trail for a handful of Cheetos Puffs. I can say this with confidence because that's what I did.

While visiting the Great Smoky Mountains National Park with my family and a handful of friends, we got the bright idea to hike up to Clingmans Dome instead of driving to it like everyone else. I'm always down for some adventure travel, but I was nervous about this hike. First of all, my fitness level at the time was severely lacking, and I knew the gain in elevation would kick my butt. I'm from Florida, which is flat as a pancake. We barely have hills. My lungs are not trained to hike anything with an incline. Not wanting to be left behind or forced to drive the car alone up that steep mountain pass, I agreed to the hike.

The first 30 minutes of the hike went something like this:

* We spent 15 minutes pulling off to the side of the road at random spots to search for the trail because it was an unofficial starting point.
* We finally made our way into the forest. I ducked and dodged every leaf I saw because I didn't know how to identify poison ivy, but I was warned to look out for it.
* We found the trail and started walking. It was relatively flat. For a few fleeting minutes, I felt confident that this hike would be a piece of cake.
* Oops! I spoke too soon. We climbed over slippery rocks and braced ourselves against trees.

I was winded and ready to turn back. Several members of my group had already slipped and fallen. This is not what I had in mind.

When we stopped for a quick water break, I sought comfort, so I reached into my backpack and pulled out a bag of Cheetos Puffs. The salty, cheesy goodness coated my tongue and sent a wave of happiness over me. That's when I came up with the idea of celebrating my progress during the hike by rewarding myself with a cheesy snack. Every time we stopped, I ate three Cheetos Puffs. It worked! By the time we made it to the top of Clingmans Dome, I was covered in orange Cheeto dust and feeling pleased that I didn't give up on the hike. So yes, I hiked a portion of the Appalachian Trail for Cheetos Puffs. Take that, Klondike Bar.

As silly as this story is, it highlights a fundamental idea: celebrating your progress, no matter the size, can influence continued action. There is real magic in celebrating your wins and rewarding yourself throughout the journey versus waiting until you reach your destination. I could have chosen to eat the Cheetos once we reached the dome, but I wouldn't have this amazing story to share with you. Besides, I might not have finished the hike. Taking those moments to celebrate my progress while rewarding myself helped me keep going.

We don't celebrate our wins, successes, o' accomplishments enough. It is a problem epidemic proportions.

And you know what? I'm guilty of it too. I'm guilty of not ꜰ to smell the roses in my field of success. I'm guilty of only on what I have yet to achieve and completely o how far I've come - the progress I've made. I want ᴜ ter. I want us to add elements of celebration to o because we are worth celebrating.

Now I know what you're thinking. "Every day'

through Sunday? Girl, that's crazy!"

It's not.

Celebrating your success and achievements every day is possible. Not only that, it's very doable. But to get to that place of daily celebrations, we have to face some ugly truths and break down commonly held misconceptions about what it means to celebrate yourself. Maybe then I'll convince you that folding your laundry straight out of the dryer is worthy of an impromptu celebratory dance party. (Spoiler alert: it is!) If you're feeling spicy, wait until I tell you that flossing twice daily allows you to double up on your daily celebrations. Even your dentist will want to celebrate with you on your next visit.

Why aren't we celebrating a whole lot more? I'm sure you have your reasons. I know I have mine. I posed this question to my friend Tami, who, by the way, is an excellent celebrater. We had a spirited conversation about this, and she shared a list of reasons her clients gave her for not celebrating. As you read them, I invite you to look inward and see if any of these rings true for you. Here are some reasons:

"I don't have time."

"I don't feel like I can slow down."

"It's not a big deal."

"I'm uncomfortable being celebrated."

"I don't want to be seen as a braggart."

While these might technically meet the criteria for being reasons, none of them feels like a good reason. Definitely not to me.

Want to know what's even more interesting? All of these reasons are just an excuse rooted in fear. You don't celebrate yourself because you are afraid.

Being alive is a vulnerable experience. Every day we have to protect ourselves against threats to our lives and overall sense of wellbeing. I explained this in Chapter 1 when I told you about the three types of fear: primal, rational, and irrational. These threats don't solely come in the form of physical danger, like bear attacks. There are threats against our mental and emotional state and livelihoods. Our defenses are up all the time.

True joyful celebration requires us to take risks. Lower our guards. It needs us to get uncomfortable, stand up to the Chorus of Fear and say, "I celebrate this." It needs us to be fully present in the moment. It demands we stop ruminating over past missteps or worrying about future problems.

Letting go of our defenses and distractions to lean into moments of joyful celebration leaves us feeling exposed. We don't like how that feels. It's uncomfortable. It feels too vulnerable. What happens if I let my guard down and the moment passes, leaving a disaster in its wake? How will I cope? That feeling of vulnerability is scary.

In the book *Daring Greatly,* Brené Brown talks about how joy is the most vulnerable emotion and introduces us to the idea of foreboding joy.

> *"Scarcity and fear drive foreboding joy. We're afraid that the feeling of joy won't last, or that we won't be enough, or that the transition to disappointment (or whatever is in store for us next) will be too difficult. We've learned that giving in to joy is, at best, setting ourselves up for disappointment and, at worst, inviting disaster. And we struggle with the worthiness issue. Do we deserve our joy, given our inadequacies and imperfections? What about the starving children and the war-ravaged world? Who are we to be joyful?"*
>
> BRENÉ BROWN

In moments when we should be celebrating how far we've come, all we seem to be able to think about is how it will all go up in smoke if we let our guard down for one second. Of all the tricks that the Chorus of Fear has pulled, filling our heads with lame excuses and robbing us of the joy of celebration is its greatest trick. It's so subtle. You don't realize that it's happening.

You're a smart cookie, and I can sense a but ready to slide off your lips. You're still not prepared to accept that your reasons for not celebrating are just excuses. Challenge accepted.

Here's why your reasons don't hold up:

"I DON'T HAVE TIME."

You can make time. A celebration doesn't need to be long. You can spare two minutes, and that's the exact time it takes to fire off a quick text to a friend sharing your celebratory news.

"I DON'T FEEL LIKE I CAN SLOW DOWN."

Slowing down is not the same thing as stopping. You can allow yourself to slow down long enough to mark your accomplishment with a celebration. Again, a celebration doesn't need to take a lot of time.

"IT'S REALLY NOT A BIG DEAL."

Life is hard. Full stop. Every day you survive living on a floating spinning space rock is a reason to celebrate. If that's not a good enough reason, then what is? Stop minimizing your achievements. Make them a big deal because if you won't, then who will?

"I'M NOT COMFORTABLE BEING CELEBRATED."

This excuse shines a light on your relationships with others. In a connected world, we have become more disconnected than ever. Social media has done a number on us. A scroll through any social network reveals a showcase of perfectly curated and filtered lives. It's painfully clear that we are unwilling to open ourselves up to be seen truly. We don't want to share our triumphs if it opens us to the possibility of having to share our losses which drags up those fears of rejection, inadequacy, and judgment.

It's time to assess whether you're inviting people into your life in a meaningful way or keeping them at an emotional arm's length. We want to celebrate with people we feel connected to. You have to be willing to invite people in to celebrate your wins and hold space for your failures, disappointments, and tragedies. It is extremely vulnerable.

I don't believe social media is the best place to celebrate. It's full of strangers sharing their highlight reels, and there's little connection. A small but mighty group of people clapping for you will do more to boost your confidence than 100 people tapping the like button. Allow yourself to be celebrated by people who are happy to celebrate you.

"I DON'T WANT TO BE SEEN AS A BRAGGART."

I hear you. We've all encountered someone who is too self-important and always bragging. It's annoying. You don't want to be that person. And you won't be. Now hear me out.

You aren't them. And celebrating your achievements with people who want to see you win isn't the same thing as bragging.

So where is the line? How do you know when you are venturing into the land of the braggarts? I believe it comes down to intention.

Are you sharing your wins to highlight a moment of your success with people who care about you? Or are you trying to one-up everyone to prove that you're better than them? There is a difference.

I don't believe we should keep our wins to ourselves. Celebrating the good stuff is how we stand up to the Chorus of Fear. In a world that can feel at times like it's devoid of anything good, sharing your happiness is a radical act. I encourage you to share more. Sharing the things you've been able to achieve signals to others what is possible for them. You become a beacon of permission and possibility for those looking for the light. Shine as bright as you can.

Excuses. Excuses. Excuses.

EXERCISE

Are you good at celebrating yourself? If not, what is your reason for not celebrating more often? Do you feel like this is a good reason?

Celebrating Fuels More Tiny Action Taking

What's the big deal with celebrating anyway? Celebrating achievements big and small is fuel for further achievement. In other words, celebrating isn't a bonus; it is the fuel powering you to your next accomplishment.

Celebrating is critical to your success. It boosts your confidence and increases motivation. It reinforces your lessons learned. And it feels terrific.

Speaking of feeling good, it isn't an accidental byproduct of celebrating. There's scientific backing that celebrating has a positive effect on your brain. Endorphins get released inside your body when you celebrate and you feel amazing. When you accomplish something and don't take the time to celebrate, you miss out on a crucial feeling that reinforces your success. Celebrating your wins not only feels great physically, but it reinforces the behavior you want to show up when you face a new challenge or opportunity.

When you don't celebrate your accomplishments, you train your brain to view what you are doing as unexciting or unimportant. Your motivation diminishes, and eventually, you treat every accomplishment as the same. Over time this results in fewer feelings of satisfaction and fulfillment, which sets the stage for burnout as you keep chasing the next goal.

People who never slow down to celebrate begin to experience achiever's amnesia. They get so used to pursuing the next thing that they don't recognize, remember or feel what they've already accomplished. They end up feeling like they aren't doing enough. They never stop to acknowledge all they've already done.

Even Beyoncé has talked about the importance of acknowledging progress. In her February 2013 interview with GQ,

Beyoncé shared that she keeps a "crazy archive" of her past performances and achievements to remind her of how far she's come professionally and personally.

Make Celebrating Easy, So You Do It More Often

If you want to make celebrating easy so that you do it more often, then you have to let it be easy. It is probably a good time to highlight the difference between celebration and rewards. They get used interchangeably even though they mean different things. The slight difference in meaning contributes to a common misconception about what it looks like to celebrate. Many of our ideas around celebrating are tied to social gatherings because we relegate celebrating to significant life moments and milestones.

Oxford Languages defines a celebration as *"the action of marking one's pleasure at an important event or occasion by engaging in enjoyable activities."* While a reward is defined as *"a thing given in recognition of one's effort or achievement."* In other words, rewards can be a part of a celebration, but not every celebration needs a reward, just enjoyable activities.

Just as the accomplishments we celebrate don't have to be large, our celebrations don't have to be grand. They don't need to be long, time-consuming, flashy, expensive, or involve public declarations. They just need to be meaningful.

One cute and noteworthy example of celebration I remember happened during the early days of launching the Visionary Journal. I got my husband and son on board to help me celebrate getting sales. Anytime they heard my phone chime cha-ching, they would fist pump. We could be in the grocery store with the sales notifications going off, and I'd glance over to see my husband fist pumping down the aisle. Our son was right behind him. It became a fun way to get my family involved in celebrating the hard work I put into growing my business. And to this day, I still fist pump when I get sales.

Meaningful celebration looks different for everyone. For some people, it might be as simple as phoning a friend to share your good news and basking in the glow of that friend's praise and acknowledgment. Maybe it's swinging by the local pizza spot to grab a tasty pizza and give yourself the night off from cooking. The idea is that you must find what feels meaningful to you.

It's worth taking the time to investigate so that you can get the most from your celebrations. If you're unsure of the type of celebration that would feel meaningful to you, a good start is by reading the book The 5 Love Languages and figuring out what your love language is. You can even take a quiz if reading another book doesn't fit your schedule right now. Once you discover your love language, you can test out ways to celebrate that highlight your love language. You might find that words of affirmation are enough or that gifts are how you like to celebrate.

Here are other ways to make celebrating your achievements easy:

Give yourself permission to feel proud of yourself. Being an adult is kind of unhinged. I've found that adults will allow themselves to feel disappointment or sadness pretty much unchecked but hold back on permitting themselves to feel pride and joy. I can only think of one word to describe this. Unhinged! Foreboding joy wins again.

Give yourself permission to let the good feelings flow in just as easily as you allow the bad ones. Stop gatekeeping joy. Of all the feelings, you should never cap joy. And if you need someone else to give you permission, I've got a gift for you: permission granted.

Savor your success. Have you ever been to a chocolate tasting? It's fascinating because the experience is multisensory. It's not solely about eating chocolate. You are encouraged to look, sniff, snap, taste, and savor it. It deepens the tasting experience making it more memorable. Can you see where I'm going with this?

When celebrating, try to savor your success by involving multiple senses. Start by allowing yourself a moment to feel all the things. Happiness, joy, pride. Feel them radiating from inside. Then, move outside your body. Feel the sun on your skin. Listen to the ambient noise around you. Finally, take a mental snapshot. Learn to savor the delicious moments of celebration by slowing down and taking it all in.

If you let celebrating be easy, you'll have fewer reasons not to do it. Now comes the real challenge, following through and celebrating yourself. Celebration for those who don't regularly celebrate requires practice. None of this works if you don't do it.

Simple Ways To Celebrate Every Day

To help you get started, I created a short list of simple ways to celebrate every day.

Share your good news with a friend or accountability group. You must do this as directly as possible, so call or text your friend. Sharing your news on social media is easier and probably faster, but you won't get the same motivational boost. You'll be too distracted by the number of likes (or lack thereof) your post receives, which kills the celebratory vibe.

Make a toast to yourself. It seems silly, but how often has someone made a toast to you? Not often enough, I promise. The next time you're at dinner with family or friends, raise a toast to your latest and greatest accomplishments.

Keep an accomplishments jar or a good news file. We all need to be reminded occasionally (or all the time, honestly) of just how far we've come. An accomplishments jar or good news file is the perfect place to tuck away your wins for those days you need a pick-me-up. I like to read through the contents of my jar on New Year's Eve as a review of all the good the year held.

Use the good dishes/ wear the expensive lipstick/ put on your best outfit. Why do we let all the good stuff gather dust and languish in the back of our closets? Don't wait for some distant milestones to use your best stuff. Use it today!

Give yourself a gold star sticker. You are always achieving, and it's a myth that you are only successful once you've reached that elusive goal. Track your progress by awarding yourself gold stars. It is the perfect excuse to hoard cute stickers from the stationery aisle.

Take a walk. I know you probably haven't considered celebrating with exercise but hear me out. It's excellent for your overall well-being. Your brain also sweetens the deal by releasing feel-good chemicals like dopamine.

Start a success journal. You don't need a fancy notebook but feel free to use starting a success journal as an excuse to buy a pretty notebook. Then, fill the pages with all your wins and gush about how awesome you are.

Take a nap. I don't believe you need to earn rest to take it, but I welcome additional nap time. Pretend you're back in Pre-K, grab your favorite blanket, and snuggle up with pinkie pie the bear while you drift off. It has the bonus of making you slow down.

Watch an episode of your favorite show guilt-free. What show is your guilty pleasure? Gift yourself up to an hour of TV minus the guilt of worrying about how else you could be spending the time.

Make a celebration playlist and dance to it. I love to sing and dance, so celebratory dance parties feel even more special. Create a playlist of songs that get you excited and your booty shaking. Find any reason to have an impromptu five-minute dance party. No celebration playlist would be complete without "Celebration" by Kool & The Gang, "Applause" by Lady Gaga, or "Happy" by Pharrell Williams. Thank me later.

Remember, to get the most out of your celebration, you should do it as soon as possible after reaching your accomplishment before moving on to your next goal.

Make A Quick Pick Celebration List

EXERCISE

The motto of daily celebration is to "let it be easy." You are more likely to participate in daily celebrations if you have a few ideas ready to execute. Make a list of 3-5 simple ways for you to celebrate. You can choose ideas from the list I shared above or develop some of your own.

_____

_____

_____

_____

_____

_____

_____

_____

Make P.L.A.N.S To Reward Yourself

When I was in the fourth grade, there was nothing that I wanted more than the Addy Walker American Girl doll. I was obsessed. Every new catalog release made me giddy. I would eagerly wait to get it in the mail. Then, I would lay on my bed propped up on my elbows and pour over the pages of the latest American Girl catalog for hours, circling everything I wanted. I fantasized about having enough money to buy the Addy doll and her many accessories. The American Girl catalog had everything—a unique doll-sized bed, outfits, and even a trunk to store Addy's things. I just knew that Addy and I were destined to have many sleepovers in our matching American Girl pajamas. The problem? American Girl dolls were expensive. I'm talking $82 for the basic doll and book combo (not to mention the cost of shipping). My mother worked full-time to provide for four kids. She was not buying me an expensive doll.

Luckily, her boyfriend was big on education and had a soft spot for me. He made a deal with me. It was simple. If I made straight-As for the entire school year, he would buy me the Addy doll.

Ok pops! Hold my Yoo-hoo! I got this! (He should have realized this was a sucker's deal. I was a straight-A student throughout elementary school.) I raced to my room, found the most recent catalog, and tore out the order form. I filled it out with my best fourth-grade handwriting and stuck it on the wall. Addy was finally going to be mine.

I left the order form tacked to my wall as a reminder of my goal and the reward I would receive once I reached it. On the final day of school, I hopped into the backseat of my mom's car, beaming from ear to ear. My last report card sporting As across the board, tucked into my backpack, waiting to be presented like a trophy. I was so pleased with myself.

Early into the summer, I finally got my Addy Walker doll—the basic set without any fancy accessories or add-ons. (Let's not get too big for our britches). It didn't matter, though. Addy was mine, and we had plenty of sleepovers. Sadly, I never did convince my mother to buy us the matching pajamas. I would buy them now, but I'm afraid I'm too big. Boo!

From a young age, I learned how rewards could help you stay motivated to finish a task or achieve a goal. But you don't have to be young to understand this. You can learn this at any age.

Here are some examples of ways to reward yourself:

* Add $25 to your travel fund if you meditate for 90% of the month
* One guilt-free evening of binge-watching your favorite show if you apply to four new jobs every week until you land one
* Buy yourself a cute new top if you go to the gym at least 12 times in one month
* Enjoy dinner at your favorite spot if you submit applications to your top three college choices before November
* Give yourself an hour to work on your hobby if you wash and fold all of your laundry by the weekend

We like receiving things for our efforts, and our brains love getting those hits of dopamine. It's a win-win, especially when you consider that the expectation of receiving a reward triggers dopamine to be released. Just the idea that a reward is coming can boost motivation, increasing the likelihood you'll follow through. You can use this to your advantage and squeak out more motivation to drive you forward.

Tami's Fear Fable

I tried hard for 40 years to be mean to myself. I got stuff done, but every step of the way was painful.

I like to set realistic goals within a short time frame. I think of them as four to six-week experiments. Very specific. I've wanted to incorporate swimming into my fitness routine for the last handful of years. I finally had access to a private pool that was heated. It is the best thing. Yet it's still hard to get out to the pool because I'm like, "Oh, but I have to do all these things."

So I decided that I was going to swim 12 times a month. Notice, I didn't say three times a week because if you miss in the first week, you're like, "Oh, the month is ruined." I stopped with the all-or-nothing thinking. It might take me until the end of the month. I might be swimming every day during those last seven days. Then, I reward myself at the end of the month.

I buy something I would have bought anyway. I just delay that gratification. I recently bought waterproof headphones so I can listen to books while swimming. Just in case you're wondering, I will be growing actual fins and gills because I'm never going to get out of the pool again.

Tami Hackbarth

The P.L.A.N.S Framework

I developed the P.L.A.N.S. framework as a resource for the Visionary Journal and other productivity tools that I've created. If you're looking for a way to keep track of your P.L.A.N.S., I invite you to visit taketinyaction.com.

(P)

Piece by piece. Tiny actions are the name of the game. Free yourself from overwhelm. Breaking down your goal or project into small action steps gives you plenty of opportunities to receive a reward.

Say your goal is to run a 5k. Here's how you can break that down:

* Download the couch to 5k training app
* Create a weekly running schedule based on app recommendations
* Jog for one minute without stopping
* Jog for three minutes without stopping
* Jog for five minutes without stopping

Lay out your rewards. Two things can make or break the effectiveness of your rewards in increasing your motivation, the reward itself and the frequency with which you receive it.

Choose rewards that are personally motivating for you, or else they won't move you to work towards them. If you love to read, it might feel motivating to buy yourself new books as a reward. Buying a book won't be a good incentive if you're only an occasional reader.

Rewards need to be given early and often, especially at the beginning. Waiting too long or requiring too much work before receiving a reward will have a negative effect. It decreases motivation.

If your goal has a longer time horizon for completion, build opportunities to reward yourself by creating milestone goals. Milestones are checkpoints that you can measure your progress against. For example, if your goal is to write a novel, one of your milestones might be to write the first 1,000 words. By using milestones, you can increase the size of your rewards as you begin to build momentum.

MILESTONE	REWARD
Write 1,000 words of my book	Fancy Frappe from Starbucks
Write 5,000 words of my book	Tacos at Taco Cat
Write three chapters of my book	Manicure
Write eight chapters of my book	Massage

Whatever you decide to do, make sure you have predetermined milestones that you're working to reach and the rewards you'll enjoy once you get there.

(A)

Analyze and track your progress. Choose the right metrics to track. Don't focus only on what goes right as you work towards your goal because things happen. Instead, pay attention to the actions you take consistently, not just if you reached the intended outcome. It might mean keeping track of the number of days in a row you've meditated, how many words you write daily, or the amount of money you're saving weekly. Tracking these types of metrics help you get closer to your goal even if you don't do things 100% perfectly.

We enjoy getting rewarded for our efforts, but progress is the most excellent motivator. When you track your progress, you can see your gains even if they aren't immediately obvious. It offers an additional splash of motivation during the early stages of your goal when it doesn't look like much is happening. It's also useful to show your progress if things drag on. You'll be able to see the data as evidence that you're getting closer.

(N)

No guilt. Follow through and reward yourself. I'm amazed at how often we delay rewarding ourselves because we feel guilty that things didn't happen as planned. You must honor your commitment to yourself because it reinforces to your brain that you can follow through on things. It helps build your trust in yourself. You've put in the work. You earned it. Enjoy your rewards.

(**S**)

Stop and review. Regular review needs to be a part of your P.L.A.N.S. I suggest you schedule a weekly meeting with yourself to review your progress. Make adjustments as needed. None of it is set in stone. If you find a particular reward isn't working, switch it for something else. If your tiny actions aren't tiny enough, make them smaller. Keep tweaking things until you find what works best for you.

Sign Your Celebration Commitment Contract

I, _____ ,
commit to taking tiny action to reach my goal. I will celebrate all my wins (big or small) and reward myself throughout my journey. I will not let fear have all the fun.

When I achieve a specific milestone, I will enjoy my chosen reward. I will fulfill the rewards without guilt or restraint.

MILESTONE	REWARD
_____	_____
_____	_____
_____	_____
_____	_____
_____	_____
_____	_____

I am committing myself to celebrating for the duration of this contract, a period of (insert timeframe).

_____

Sign and date.

_____

ADVICE #6

Key Takeaways

1. Celebrate your progress no matter the size. Celebration influences continued action.

2. When you don't celebrate your achievements, it trains your brain to view what you are doing as unexciting or unimportant.

3. Celebrations don't need to be long, time-consuming, flashy, expensive or involve public declarations. They just need to be meaningful.

4. Implement the P.L.A.N.S. framework to help you create a reward system.

130

ADVICE #7:

Find And Build Your Cheer Squad

"Yup! You are definitely pregnant."

Those were the words the nurse spoke as she entered the exam room, the door shutting silently behind her. She was so cheery and calm—no edge to her voice. Meanwhile, I wanted to throw up but not from morning sickness. I never experienced morning sickness once throughout my pregnancy. I was nauseous because the news she had just delivered was not what I wanted to hear. She confirmed the niggling suspicion that I had been ignoring for weeks. How was I going to tell my parents?

I was in the fall of my sophomore year of college when I discovered I was pregnant. While I was well aware of how babies are made, I was shocked because a baby wasn't in alignment with my college plans. Up until that point, I had done everything right. Good grades. Scholarships. I was living independently. Now I had the impending arrival of a baby to plan. I was worried about how I was going to finish school. Would I be able to graduate on time? Could I afford to take care of a child? I was a broke college student.

Torn over what I should do, I called my Grandma Coffee. My grandmother is the most religious person that I know. I expected her to express her disappointment in me or tell me that having an abortion wasn't an option. She did neither of those things. Instead, she responded with compassion. She didn't twist what was happening to me into a moral failing. She didn't make it about religion at all. She made it a question of what I thought I could handle. Could I handle this?

By the time I hung up the phone, I knew I would keep it. I was having a baby. I had no plan. No money. No idea how I was going to do it. I just knew I'd figure out a way to make it work.

Thankfully, when I felt most stressed about what was to come, I received a seemingly endless supply of support. Everyone in my life stepped up. They all played a role that helped me accomplish my goal of graduating from college on time. My dad let me move back home. My bonus mom watched my son so I could work part-time and continue attending school. My siblings became the best uncles and aunts to my little boy. My girlfriends became like a sisterhood offering lots of laughs and emotional support as I navigated the transition from college student to single mom. It was a wild time. One that I know I'll share fully in another book someday.

I've been fortunate to receive the same level of support as I've moved through different stages of my life. Whether by family, friends, or coworkers, someone has always been there to help me celebrate the good times, offer an encouraging word during the dark times, or hug me when I've needed it.

I am well supported.

So much so that I credit my success in life to having a fantastic support system. It is the secret to my success: having a support system that has my back.

My support system is my cheer squad because, like cheerleading, it's a team sport, everyone has a role, and they're essential. Have you watched a cheerleading competition? During stunts, flyers can't go up or down safely without the help of bases or spotters. Like an actual cheer team, versatile members of your cheer squad should be able to fill any role needed and be an asset to the team.

My husband is the captain of my cheer squad. I have family members that are always willing to step in and a circle of friends who feel more like family than friends. I have no shortage of support. I don't take this for granted. I'm grateful that I can always get what I need from the support system of family and friends I have built around me.

I know this isn't the case for everyone. Fortunately, creating a support system that embraces you fully and helps you reach your goals is possible. (More to come on that soon.) It comes down to one thing, surrounding yourself with people who will not only cheer you on but are happy to do so.

You Need People

There aren't many things that get under my skin, but it irks me when someone says, "I don't have friends. I don't like people like that." It's no wonder your support system is probably in shambles. That is a bad take.

Humans are not meant to do life alone.

Psychologist Abraham Maslow touched on this in his highly referenced paper *A Theory of Human Motivation* detailing a five-tier model of basic human needs. The model represented as a pyramid is now known as *Maslow's Hierarchy of Needs*.

Guess what lies smack dab in the middle of that pyramid?

Belongingness and love.

After our physiological (food, water, and rest) and safety needs are met, we have to fulfill our emotional need for relationships and being a part of a group.

I need people. You need people. We all need people. Everyone does. Some get by with a handful of people, while others have entire networks. Our journeys through life take us through various stages, and we need different types of support at each point, like finding a mentor to help us advance our career, joining a new parent's group, or leaning on existing friends as we enter college.

It's through the help of those support systems that we can build resilience in difficult times. Even times of great accomplishment require support. If you have big dreams and aspirations, you will need help.

It is why I don't subscribe to the idea of being self-made. I don't believe it exists. It's a misnomer. No one is truly self-made. The word itself implies that you've achieved success all by yourself. In my experience, there is always someone behind the scenes - a partner, coach, friend, mentor, teacher, accountability group, someone offering their support and pushing you to keep going. Success isn't achieved in a silo. Neither is being self-made.

Tyler's Fear Fable

I started my career as a news producer, and by the end of the first week, I knew it was time to go. I was a part of a group of women at work who were dealing with their own faith walks and looking for new ways to grow personally and professionally. One of the women came up with the idea of doing a Bible study during our lunch hour.

We have Bible study one afternoon, and when it is time for prayer requests, my third executive producer says, "I'd like to pray for Tyler." As she prayed, she said, "I just want God to direct her. Make her path straight. She has a lot weighing on her. She has a lot of decisions she needs to make. God, just fill her with your boldness and your confidence."

The following day, all hell breaks loose. I was on-air producing a segment. I finally got fed up. So I went into the bathroom right before my segment. I look in the mirror and say, "God, I am tired of doing this. I'm tired of crying about this job. I'm tired of praying about this job. You have to do something today. I need you to move."

I heard the voice of God tell me, "I have something greater for you." I went to my desk, did my segment, and finished my show. Then I went back to my computer and typed a three-sentence resignation letter.

I have not looked back. That was five years ago.

The catalyst for that decision wasn't necessarily that I was feeling uncomfortable. It wasn't that I knew it was time to go. It was the Bible study where my executive producer said, "I need God to help my friend."

People around me realized that I was unhappy. They realized that I wasn't living up to my potential. Sometimes it's the strength of other people that pushes us into our destiny. Fear is very crippling. Having a tribe of people who can see those things in you is vital. They will have your back. I firmly believe that God has already called the people who are here to help you.

Tyler Young

One cheat code for dealing with the Chorus of Fear is having a solid support system for yourself. Coping with fear can make you feel alone or isolated. Your support system might be the welcome voice of encouragement you need when the Chorus of Fear starts singing too loudly.

If you want to make bold moves in your life, you need to find good members for your cheer squad. You don't need seat fillers or coattail riders. You need genuine connections. You need people who will:

* Challenge you to put your best ideas into the world. The ones that seem wildly impossible are a little crazy and very scary to think about.
* Hold you accountable for what you said you would do. Did you reach out to that editor at the New York Times?
* Call you on your stuff when they know you're playing too small.
* Hold space for you when things get rough or the fear feels too heavy to carry because it does eventually.
* Act as a sounding board when trying to solve a problem.
* Help you be your brightest self while reminding you not to let fear have all the fun.

I know this is a tall order. Thankfully your support doesn't have to come from only one person or source. It's better to spread your support needs across multiple people or areas of your life. You need an entire cheer squad of people, and you can build one for yourself.

How To Assemble Your Cheer Squad

Hold up! Before you run off to hold tryouts for spots on your cheer squad, you must do some prep work. Your cheer squad needs to match your unique needs, goals, strengths, and weaknesses to work effectively. You need to know some critical things about yourself to assess whether certain people will be a good fit.

Identify Your S.Q.U.A.D. Goals

"Knowing yourself is the beginning of all wisdom."
ARISTOTLE

I'd have to agree with Aristotle. After all, he is one of the greatest philosophers of all time. Knowing yourself, especially your skills and weaknesses, help you figure out what you need from a support system. To be most effective, your cheer squad should complement your skills, qualities, unique interests, aspirations, and deficiencies, otherwise known as your S.Q.U.A.D. goals. After you identify your S.Q.U.A.D. goals, you'll have clarity on where you are now and where you ultimately want to go. Then, you can better see who is best suited to offer you support.

The reality of life is that you will experience many different events and challenges. You can't expect one or two people to be available and ready to support you through all of them. Figuring out your needs in different areas of your life and then knowing who to reach out to for help makes your cheer squad more effective. Once you identify your S.Q.U.A.D goals, you'll better understand where you could most use support and how you can be a good source of support for others.

Let's break down each piece:

SKILLS

Skills are the things you do well. Everyone possesses a variety of different skills and talents. Having an eye for design, building birdhouses, and learning to manage projects at work. Some skills are natural. Others are learned through experience and education. How they came about isn't important. What is, is knowing what you are skilled at doing.

Ask yourself:

- What are my skills?
- What are my natural abilities or talents?
- How could I use my skills to enhance my support system?

QUALITIES

Your personal qualities are the characteristics that make up who you are. Goal-driven. Sensitive. Optimistic. Kind. Quiet. These defining traits lay the foundation of the type of person you are. When looking for cheer squad members, you might seek out people with similar or complementary qualities.

Ask yourself:

- What characteristics do I believe define who I am?
- What qualities do I possess that would be useful in a group?
- What are my strengths?

UNIQUE INTERESTS

Unique interests are things you want to know or learn more about, like hobbies. Identifying your interests is helpful because it can expose you to a community outside your current circle. Your interests can foster stronger relationships with people you might not normally consider connecting with.

Ask yourself:

* What are my interests?
* What topics can I chat about for hours without getting bored?
* What topics would I like to go deeper on?

ASPIRATIONS

Aspirations are things you hope to achieve or accomplish. Climbing a mountain, getting promoted to manager, or owning an ice cream parlor are a few examples that come to mind.

Ask yourself:

* Where would I like to see myself personally or professionally 6 months from now? A year from now?
* What are my goals, dreams, or vision?
* What am I working on right now?

DEFICIENCIES

No one likes to point out their weaknesses. Owning your deficiencies isn't a bad thing. When you're aware of your weak areas, you can understand what you need or how you need support.

Ask yourself:

* What are my weaknesses?
* What do I need help with?
* Where do I get stuck?

Identify Your S.Q.U.A.D. Goals

EXERCISE

Fill in the chart with details about your skills, qualities, unique interests, aspirations, and deficiencies. Once you have your S.Q.U.A.D. goals figured out, you can use that information to find cheer squad members to complement them.

S KILLS
What are my skills? Or natural abilities?

_____
_____
_____
_____
_____

Q UALITIES
What characteristics do I believe define who I am?

_____
_____
_____
_____
_____

UNIQUE INTERESTS
What are my interests?

_____
_____
_____
_____
_____

ASPIRATIONS
What are my goals, dreams, or vision?

_____
_____
_____
_____
_____

DEFICIENCIES
What are my weaknesses? Where do I get stuck?

_____
_____
_____
_____
_____

Find Your Cheer Squad Members

Now that you have an idea of your support needs based on your S.Q.U.A.D. goals; you can start looking for cheer squad members to fill in the gaps.

START CLOSE TO HOME

You don't need to look far to find your initial cheer squad members. You can start with existing family and friends. Your family and friends know you well, making them the perfect cheerleader. Who better to call when you need a boost after a tough day?

If you've let some of these relationships languish, now is the time to reach out and reconnect. These relationships already exist, but they need strengthening. With friends who live nearby, you can suggest coffee dates or a fun outing like visiting a museum. For friends and family who are farther away, phone calls, video chats, or visits will do the trick.

EMBRACE YOUR INTERESTS

What activities do you enjoy? Are you a crafter, enjoy theater, or a basketball fanatic? Your interests are an excellent way to connect with like-minded souls in your community. Clubs and community spaces exist for nearly every type of interest. You just need a little boldness to attend local events. Try joining a movie club or a kickball team.

Don't worry if you are not instantly flooded with new friend requests. Friendships take time to build, so be consistent and keep showing up. Even if you don't meet your new best friend, you still reap the benefits of a stress-relieving activity — a truly underrated perk of building your support system.

INCREASE YOUR PROFESSIONAL NETWORK

If you have big career ambitions and want to climb the corporate ladder, a strong professional support system is crucial. Coworkers are cool, but things can get tricky once you start exploring new career opportunities outside your current company.

To develop this network, look to build relationships inside and outside your company. Consider attending meetups for professionals, happy hours, and other networking events.

USE SOCIAL NETWORKS TO HELP EXPAND YOUR NETWORK

We live in the digital age in an increasingly digital world. You can meet people who live literally on the other side of the world. Don't discount social networks as a reliable way to connect and expand your network. I've met some of my favorite people thanks to social media. Many of them I speak to regularly but have only met in person once or twice, if at all. Our relationships are just as important as friendships I've made in person.

A good way to meet people online is to look for people or groups with similar interests. In the online world, there is a flavor for everyone, so don't be afraid of using the search bar.

Start your search by using words that describe your interest in the most obvious and broad terms—photographers, Jeep lovers, or boba tea. I suggest additional searches using broad terms paired with specific descriptors like women photographers or Florida Jeep lovers. Review the search results for interesting people or community pages. Follow or join the ones that interest you.

Then, you can engage with people through comments. Respond to their posts and like their stuff. Leave thoughtful replies. Eventually, if you feel the vibe is right, ask them if they'd be interested in setting up a virtual coffee chat. It is not a pick-your-brain session. It's an opportunity to connect and discover what else you have in common besides a shared interest online. Again, keep an open mind if your new friend isn't blowing up your messages after your initial chat. Good friendships take time.

Who Ya Gonna Call?

EXERCISE

Each cheer squad member plays an important support role in your life. For each description, fill in the name of the person best suited to provide that type of support to you.

Will offer me career advice

_____

Will give me a pep talk on a rough day

_____

Will hold me accountable

_____

Will offer me general life advice

_____

Will be happy to talk about my hobby/interest

_____

Melissa's Fear Fable

I've always wanted to write. I've had a bunch of private blogs, but I've never shared them with anyone. I was afraid of what people would think about me expressing my ideas.

I'm the only person within my friend group doing stuff like this. So saying, "I can't hang out" because I'm working on my blog felt uncomfortable. I think I feared losing friends.

To be completely honest, my family was the least supportive. I would be excited about something I accomplished, and they'd say, "Oh, okay." To me, it felt like they were blowing it off. That's when I realized the people around me may not be interested in what I'm doing because it's not what interests them. So I found a blogging clique.

Blogging is a single-person activity. It can be lonely if you're always doing it alone. Finding a community of other women blogging and creating new friendships based on our shared interests was cool. I grew my friendship circle.

Now when I have conversations about blogging, I have people who are also excited about it. They can relate. We can talk about WordPress or whatever, and it's never a boring conversation. We sit and share ideas.

Melissa Allen

Get Your Squad In Formation

Once you've got your cheer squad together, it's time to make it work. A healthy support system includes:

Accountability. Give your cheer squad permission to hold you accountable for what you say that you will do or who you strive to become. Allowing others to hold you accountable can mean many things—calling your bluff when needed, offering honest feedback, and helping you stay or get back on track.
Important Note: If you want accountability, ensure you are willing to receive it. Relationships can become strained if your responses to someone holding you accountable become hostile.

Fellowship. Make room in your schedule and life to speak or meet with members of your squad regularly. Plan check-ins and give updates. You don't have to limit yourself to only discussing your latest win or the next goal. Leave space to chat about what you're watching on Netflix or a recently discovered album.

A sense of purpose. Everyone has a purpose in life. Your cheer squad should be there to help you accomplish your life's purpose, or if you haven't figured it out, they should help you realize yours.

Self-care. Sure, this chapter has mostly been about how others can support you, but it's essential to know how to support yourself. You have a responsibility to ensure that you are okay. Make supporting yourself a top priority by practicing self-care. Check in with yourself to see how you are doing. Invest time into doing things that refill your cup. Rest when you need it. Book an appointment with your therapist. Self-care is more than just manicures and bubble baths.

Be A Good Cheerleader For Others

Picture this. It's the middle of the day, and I'm on a cruise ship in the middle of the ocean. I'm standing on stage in front of a small audience of people doing karaoke and fumbling my way through UGK's "Int'l Players Anthem." I'm not sure why I chose this song. The rapping is way too fast for me to keep up. In my head, I know most of Andre 3000's opening verse. In reality, I'm shaky, rapping it out loud, fumbling, and mumbling my way through the words.

> *"Keep your heart three stacks, keep your heart*
> *Aye, keep your heart three stacks, keep your heart*
> *Man, these girls is smart, three stacks, these girls is smart*
> *Play your part"*
>
> ANDRE 3000,
"Int'l Players Anthem (I choose you)"

The beat drops.

And for one long moment, time slows. I look out into the crowd. There's a wave of people. Smiling, rapping, and bopping to the beat while wearing t-shirts that read "Caution: We on a boat" printed across the chest. The energy is so infectious. I don't finish the song. I mean, I was struggling through it anyway. So I walk off stage to join the crowd. As we laugh and continue to dance with the sound of UGK playing in the background, I know I've found my people. My cheer squad. People who have embraced me, laughed with me, cried with me, and performed bad karaoke with me.

I want you to be surrounded by people who want the best for you. People who will allow you to lean on them during challenging times and help you celebrate when things are going well. As I stated earlier, my cheer squad is the key to my success, but receiving that level of support doesn't just happen.

It isn't accidental.

In most cases, having people as a part of your support system makes you a default member of theirs. Building your cheer squad is just as much about what you put into those relationships as what you get out of them. That is why you must learn to be a supportive cheerleader for others.

Curious about what that might look like? I thought you might be, so I wrote this list of 7 ways that you can be a supportive cheerleader for others.

1. FIND JOY IN THEIR SUCCESSES

Freudenfreude is a German word that means "finding enjoyment in another's success." If ever there was a word to accurately describe the role of a cheerleader to a sports team, freudenfreude would be it.

Freudenfreude is peak cheerleader energy. Whenever their team scores, cheerleaders celebrate, show excitement, and invite others to join in. They make the members of their team feel good through celebration.

One meaningful way to be a good cheerleader for your squad is to be genuinely happy and find joy in their success. Buy their favorite dessert to celebrate with them, gush excitedly about their achievements to other squad members, or call to say how proud you are of them.

Joy is contagious. Don't be afraid to spread it.

2. GIVE AS MUCH AS YOU TAKE

Support systems, like many other types of relationships, are a two-way street. There's an ebb and flow, yin and yang. A balance is struck between the giver and whoever is on the receiving end. It's selfish to expect other people to support or cheer you on, and when it's their turn in the spotlight, you barely have a word to offer them. You must reciprocate the supportive energy that is offered to you. Try your best to make sure there's an even exchange of energy. Don't hog the support because it's not only about you.

3. BE A CONNECTOR

Keep an eye out for people you can connect with members of your support system. Making connections leads to conversations, which can bring beneficial things like new friendships and opportunities. Being a good connector enriches not only your network but the network of the connection as well.

For example, I have a friend, Jodel, who is an excellent connector. He seems to know everyone and is constantly introducing me to new people. The thing that makes him such a good connector is that he's always trying to bring people together. He finds joy in having good company, and the result of that is a full circle of like-minded friends who bring a variety of different views and experiences. He's not afraid to greet and invite strangers to his table for a drink.

4. BUILD THEIR CONFIDENCE

Confidence is an important indicator of success. People who lack confidence rarely thrive. They see more risks than opportunities. That means confidence can make or break people's ability to achieve their goals. Unfortunately, we can't snap our fingers and become more confident, but you can help build up less confident members of your squad. Give them compliments. Ask them to share their advice. Give them the chance to take the lead on activities. Do your best to instill confidence in all members of your cheer squad. Remember: you should not be the only person on your cheer squad winning.

5. HAND OUT PRAISE AND RECOGNITION OFTEN

Everyone likes to be recognized for their efforts. Your cheer squad is no exception. When you notice someone doing well, praise and affirm them and let them know you see them. Recognize them in front of their peers. Be generous with praise and recognition. It costs zero dollars, so there's no reason to hold back.

6. SHOW EMPATHY

Life has its ups and downs. While we prefer the ups, there will be times when you'll help weather life's storms with your squad. Showing empathy is important because it helps you understand how others feel so you can respond appropriately to the situation.

For instance, when a cheer squad member experienced the loss of their grandmother, I coordinated with a few other members to send flowers for the funeral service because we couldn't attend in person. Later she told me that it made her feel good to know her friends thought of her during a difficult time.

I picked up this idea from my favorite cousin Elizabeth who sent me a care package of magazines, coloring books, and markers when I was in the hospital. Small gestures speak volumes.

7. ASK THEM, "HOW CAN I HELP?"

Seek opportunities to offer your support to members of your cheer squad. Even within our support systems, some people are afraid, don't know how, or don't want to inconvenience others by asking for help. Usually, these are our biggest helpers and supporters (because, of course, they are). Relieve the pressure by asking how you can help them. Allow them the chance to receive support without needing to ask for it. Even if they don't have issues with asking, everyone loves to receive help without always asking, "Will you help me?"

ADVICE #7

Key Takeaways

1. To be most effective, your cheer squad should complement your skills, qualities, unique interests, aspirations, and deficiencies, otherwise known as your S.Q.U.A.D. goals.

2. You can find members for your cheer squad in various places: online, at work, or closer to home with family members and friends.

3. Support is a two-way street. Make sure you're offering the level of support you expect to receive to other cheer squad members.

SCIENCE
YES!

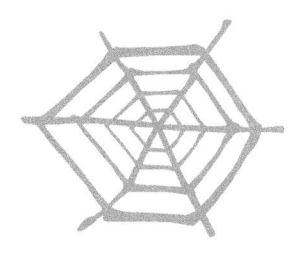

ADVICE #8:

Treat Failure As An Event, Not An Endpoint

I used to take daily morning walks with my husband around a nice three-mile loop through our neighborhood. It was gorgeous. I'd watch the sunrise and bathe everything in its golden light. There weren't too many cars rushing by yet.

Along our route, there was a stretch that passed through several large oak trees. Spinybacked Orbweaver spiders lived in those trees, and when the sun caught the drops of dew on their webs just right, you could see how big they were. Spinybacked Orbweavers is their scientific name, but I call them crab spiders because they look like tiny crabs. They are relatively small spiders, so I was always impressed with how large a web they built. The webs stretched between the trees' gaps and extended to the ground.

Each day, as I walked by, I would say aloud some variation of, "Wow, look how big that one is" or "OMG! Can you believe that the web can touch the ground?"

My husband's response was always the same, "You gotta build a big web to get what you want."

The first time I heard him say it, I was startled at how simple and profound his answer was. I saved it as a voice note on my phone.

You gotta build a big web to get what you want. You need to repeat this mantra when the Chorus of Fear starts warming up.

Build A Big Web

There it is, friend. Too many people seem to miss this step on their quest to go after what they want and live a bolder life. You have to give your best effort to get what you want. Who knew it was hiding in the trees?

The quirk about going after what you want means you must put in the work and effort upfront. I'm not talking about a half-baked effort. It has to be good. The best effort that you are capable of right now. Afterward, you wait patiently for that big juicy fly to land on your web.

If you are lucky, you catch something right away. A fly. A moth. A wasp. But we're not always that lucky. And this is where it gets tricky; most of the time, you will have to repair your web after something comes along and pokes holes in it. Or tears it down completely.

You are going to fail to catch a fly a lot. But it's ok. You still don't get to reduce your effort, though. You build your biggest and best web all over again.

To a spider, failing to catch a fly today is an opportunity to try again tomorrow. Do not give up. You don't know which attempt to catch a fly will work out. But each time, you have the chance to make a better web using the information you learned from your previous attempts.

Failure doesn't mean your idea isn't valid or your dream isn't good enough. Failure simply means there's a lesson to be learned or another direction to take. Failure won't kill you, but your fear of failing might keep you from succeeding. You can learn more from a single failure than from a lifetime of success.

Redefine What It Means To Fail

Have you ever been so afraid of failing at something that you decided not to try?

The concept of failure has done a number on us. We read way too much into it. It's so loaded, more loaded than a Wendy's baked potato. The idea of failing and what it means was conditioned into you from childhood. It traces back to how you were taught to measure success.

What type of messages about failure and success did you receive? Were you taught to measure your success by a variety of different factors? Or were you taught that there is only one possible route to success? One goal, one correct path, and one outcome.

If you were taught the latter, you probably believe falling short of achieving your goal means failing. And then what happens? You attach meaning to it, like failing makes you a failure. It diminishes your sense of self-worth and destroys your self-esteem. You start to believe yourself to be a failure.

What I find interesting about this is that most of the expectations you fail to meet are ones you've created. You are the one setting the goalpost for what failure is. You don't have to accept the misguided definition of failure that you've been taught. You can define what failure means to you so that it works to motivate you.

How do you define failure? What does failure look like to you? When do you actually fail?

These are questions that you probably haven't given much thought to. I want you to develop your own guidelines for what failure means to you. Give this some deep thought. That way, you will recognize it when you experience it.

I know I've failed when:

* I did not bother to try.
* I quit at the first sign of difficulty.
* I will not accept anything less than perfect execution, especially when I'm learning something new.
* I haven't taken the opportunity to try again.
* I haven't surrendered to the process.

You aren't going to knock every goal out of the park. It's unrealistic to expect that, but you'll get closer with each attempt. Start treating failure as an event, not an endpoint. Having a definition for failure you've created for yourself is the best way to take the sting out of falling short of reaching your goal.

Define What Failure Means To You

EXERCISE

I've shared what failure means and how I define it. Now it's your turn. Write your definition of failure. What does failure look like for you? How do you know when you've failed? Describe it in enough detail that you're clear about when you've failed.

Failure Vs. Setback

I know I just made you go through the process of defining a failure for yourself, but I have an even more provocative question for you. Was it a failure? Or did you experience a setback?

I've learned that what we view as failure is just a gap in our perception. We've misinterpreted the information because as long as you keep taking steps forward and making progress, you aren't failing. You've confused a failure with a setback.

A setback is a deviation from your intended path to success. It is a learning opportunity to propel you forward, not a stop sign.

I've experienced plenty of setbacks in my life. I'm sure you have too. One particularly vivid example was transitioning from chemically straightened hair (aka a relaxer) to my natural curls. You would think this wouldn't be a big deal, but I received my first relaxer at age six. I didn't know how to take care of or style curly hair. It took three attempts over several years before wearing my curly hair stuck.

Each time the same thing would happen. I'd reach a point where I believed I was ready to embrace my natural curls. I'd go get my "big chop" cutting off my chemically straightened hair, spend a day or two freaking out, and end up back at the salon getting another relaxer. If you've seen me rocking a random pixie cut at some point, this is why.

The lesson learned that helped my third attempt work out was realizing that I needed to cut my hair into a style that felt like me and eased me into the change. New hair routine. New products. In my previous attempts, I'd chop off my hair and experience shock because I couldn't see myself walking around like that. It wasn't a failure. It was a setback because I learned an important lesson that helped me achieve my goal. I haven't had a relaxer since 2010.

It is an excellent place to mention that there isn't a time limit on trying again. Going natural didn't happen right away. It took me years to figure it out. You live, you learn, and you try again with better information.

Plenty of famous people and historical figures experienced setbacks in their younger years and used them to find success later in life. Here are a few of my favorites:

Michael Jordan was cut from his high school basketball team because his coach didn't think he had enough skill. He later went on to win an NCAA national championship and six NBA championships with the Chicago Bulls.

Lady Gaga was signed to Island Def Jam Records, only to get dropped after three months. She later found success at Interscope Records.

Vera Wang's original dream was to be a professional figure skater, but she didn't make the U.S. Olympic team in 1986. Years later, she worked as an editor at Vogue magazine before becoming one of the most recognized fashion designers in the world.

Oprah Winfrey was fired as an evening news reporter at Baltimore's WJZ-TV. She's now a household name and the undisputed queen of daytime television.

Beyoncé Knowles-Carter as a member of the singing group Girls Tyme lost when they performed on Star Search. She later led the R&B group Destiny's Child and became a successful solo artist selling out venues worldwide.

After reading each of those scenarios, do you consider them to be failures or merely setbacks?

Unless it's impossible to try again, don't get too hung up on failure. It's not proof you need to stop. It's a setback. A roadblock to be navigated around. Don't read more into it than that. Actual failure only happens when you stop trying. Quitting means fear has all the fun. It wins.

Christopher's Fear Fable, Part 1

I was nervous because it was my first time trying out for any organized sport. Up until the tryouts, I had only played basketball with the kids in P.E. I didn't think I was that bad, but it was a different story when it came time for tryouts.

I tried out for the seventh and eighth-grade basketball teams. I thought I did pretty well. The coach thought otherwise. When I checked the list of people who made the team, I didn't see my name. I was extremely disappointed. I didn't cry, but I wanted to. (Note from Monique: Our dad said he cried.)

I wanted to play basketball but didn't know enough about it. I was afraid because I'd already failed at it by not making the team. So I turned to the one person I felt could help me, my dad. He's always been a basketball junkie.

He trained me pretty rigorously. Signed me up for organized basketball leagues. I'm not going to lie; I was by far the worst player on my team and got teased.

I felt the fear again. But my dad always told me, "If you keep practicing and doing what you're supposed to do, you're going to pass all those guys. And they won't be laughing anymore."

No one laughed when I made the team the following year.

Christopher Malcolm

How To Reset After Experiencing A Setback

Let's talk about navigating a setback for a moment, shall we?

In setting goals, building a business, or creating our big, bold lives, you will experience a setback at some point. It's easy to stay motivated when things are going well and you're getting the intended results. On the other hand, a setback will make you question whether or not it's worth it to continue. The answer is YES! Honestly, setbacks are just another unavoidable part of the human experience.

Even though it may not feel like it at the moment, setbacks are survivable. You'll come out on the other side feeling a little stronger and more confident. Until you get to that place, here are a few tips to help you navigate the uncomfortable waters of a setback.

ALLOW YOURSELF SOME GRACE

Do you remember Tami from Chapter 6? When I interviewed her, she told me, "If being mean to ourselves worked, we would all be perfect by now." I think this sentiment applies perfectly here. Beating yourself up about not reaching a goal isn't helpful. Give yourself some grace.

Sometimes our best-laid plans don't pan out. Life happens. We get sick. Our circumstances change. It's disappointing. It's heartbreaking. It's really easy to get discouraged. Just because things didn't happen during the timeline we laid out for them doesn't mean they won't happen.

DO OTHER ACTIVITIES YOU ENJOY

Experiencing a setback takes the wind from your sails. It leaves you feeling deflated. Build yourself back up by doing activities that you enjoy. Do you love to read? Then allow yourself to dive into a new book. If baking is your jam, whip up your favorite recipes to enjoy alone or share. Find activities that restore you. It is time to be very intentional about practicing self-care.

LEAN ON YOUR CHEER SQUAD

Call up your cheer squad. Let them know that you've experienced a setback and that you need additional support. Your inner circle can support you by being available to listen, soundboard your feelings, hold space, or offer encouragement once you're ready to try again. Providing a much-needed boost to your motivation. Don't try to navigate your setback alone. Lean on a few people that you trust.

REFLECT ON PAST SUCCESSES

A setback does not define your potential for experiencing future success. You've experienced success in many areas of your life previously. It will happen again. Give yourself time. Feel confident about things you've already accomplished.

EASE BACK INTO IT

When you feel ready to start again, don't try to rush back into it. Take tiny steps of action. Don't feel discouraged if you don't bounce back right away. Again, things take time. Just keep taking the next small step.

A setback is not confirmation that it will never happen. A setback can be a setup for something greater.

During these times, you have to guard your energy, reassess your priorities and accept that you've done the best you can for now. You have to learn to be okay with cutting yourself some slack.

Christopher's Fear Fable, Part 2

I was well on my way to my basketball career. I'd gone from being cut from the seventh-grade team to being one of the best freshman players at my high school.

Then at the beginning of my sophomore year, before the season started, I was involved in a freak accident while playing basketball during P.E. I dislocated my left knee and broke my right ankle. I was in a wheelchair for months. I had to go through physical therapy. So the year I was supposed to come out of my shell and start making a name for myself, I spent it rehabbing a traumatic injury.

I'd worked so hard and realized this could be a career-ending injury. It was a different kind of fear. Unlike anything I had experienced. I kept thinking that if I was able to go from zero basketball skills to reaching maybe 20% of my potential within two years, how could I let this injury stop me?

Because of rehab, I missed about 90% of my sophomore year of playing basketball. But I was so hungry to get back onto that court that I did everything I could to get healed and healthy.

I already had enough standing in my way, and I wasn't going to let any excuses hold me back. At that point, basketball was my life. There's no way I was going to give that up. Even the fear couldn't stop me because I had already seen glimpses of hope that I could make a successful career out of basketball.

Christopher Malcolm

Know When To Call It Quits

Before I became a writer, podcaster, graphic designer, and a whole bunch of other titles, I was a claims adjuster at a well-known insurance company. (I won't say which one, but you could save 15% or more by switching to them.) What was once an exciting career opportunity with plenty of room for advancement quickly became a nightmare.

A year into my career, I realized claims adjusting wasn't for me. Too much pressure, micromanagement, and many claims-related nightmares sent me back into the job hunt. I decided to change careers and become a teacher. Word reached the big boss that I might be leaving the company, so he scheduled a meeting with me to discuss it. During the meeting, I told him I was going to be a teacher, to which he replied, "I don't think you'll like it. I think leaving would be a mistake."

That meeting ended with him requesting that I don't make any decisions about leaving before talking with him first. I was embarrassed and annoyed. Then, it hit me. Wait. A. Minute. Did this dude think I needed his permission to quit?

We didn't have another meeting. I left the company a few weeks later and became a middle school science teacher.

So here it is, the big reveal that I've been working up to this entire chapter. You've finally reached the point where I tell you that quitting is okay.

Gasp!

I realize this goes against all the wisdom you picked up during your early childhood watching Sesame Street and Saturday morning cartoons. Winners never quit; quitters never win. Or, however that slogan goes.

I am a quitter.

I want to go on record and let you know I've quit plenty of

things. More than a few…

I quit being a middle school teacher. Yes, the same job my former boss warned me not to take. It turns out he was right, but who cares. I learned a crucial piece of data. Middle school is a tough age. Being a middle school teacher is a career that people are called to, and I am not one of the chosen ones. I'll leave it at that.

I quit my fashion blog.

I quit my first business, Antisparkle Apparel. It was my baby. I grew it from a tiny Etsy shop to a thriving indie brand. Then, one day I realized that I had outgrown it. It no longer served me. I was afraid, but I knew that Antisparkle Apparel had fulfilled its role in my story. I quit, and I don't regret it.

I've quit being in relationships with men I only sort of liked. Then, I found one that I liked and married him. (Hey boo!)

I've quit friendships. Some were harder than others.

I quit pursuing a second bachelor's degree in journalism. I added about $20k to my overall student loan debt with nothing to show.

I quit my gym.

Quitting isn't always negative. Sometimes it's necessary. There are many reasons why it might be time for you to call it quits. You can quit to give yourself more time to grow, lower stress, or align better with your greater purpose. Maybe you've gone so far off track that quitting is the only way to find your way back.

Quitting is another part of the data-gathering process. Every time you try, you learn new ways to proceed. When you quit, you learn what happens when you're no longer attached to the actual outcome.

I've quit enough things in my life to feel comfortable sharing this wisdom with you. If you feel the desire to quit sitting like a lump of lead in your gut, it is most definitely time to quit. Trust your intuition.

Other times you know it's time to quit when...

The amount of frustration you're experiencing is greater than the reward. It is normal to have occasional moments of frustration, but there isn't much of a reward if you have to be at your wit's end all the time to receive it. You aren't only weighing risk versus benefit. You need to look at whether or not the reward is worth the frustration that you feel.

Your decision to keep going is based more on fear or avoiding judgment than anything else. Are you continuing to keep going solely out of a sense of responsibility? Afraid to admit you made a wrong choice or to start over? Don't think of quitting as either good or bad or a reflection of your self-worth. Many of us have a hard time quitting.

You've fallen victim to sunk-cost-fallacy. Sunk-cost-fallacy is the belief that you can't quit something because of all the time, money, or effort you've already invested. This type of thinking is what makes quitting so difficult. The fallacy prevents you from realizing the best choice is to do whatever promises a better experience in the future, not which negates the feeling of loss in the past.

Your physical or mental well-being is disrupted. My job as a claims adjuster used to give me literal nightmares. I would have dreams about the customers who called and harassed me constantly. That was a significant indicator that it was time to go. Disruptions to your physical and mental health are too high of a price to pay.

You feel like it. No explanation is necessary.
It is an excellent place to insert another helpful piece of wisdom:

You don't need anyone's permission to quit.

In my insurance story from earlier, you may have understood that my boss felt I needed his permission to leave a job that I wasn't happy with. Um. Who told him that?

Ironically enough, isn't that how we have been raised? To ask for permission before making drastic decisions? You are taught to seek permission from your parents or trusted adults as a child. Once you are ready to make your own decisions, you are stuck in a cycle of feeling like you need permission. And when you aren't asking directly, you are seeking approval for your choices which is still a form of asking for permission.

You don't need anyone's permission to live the big vibrant life you want to live.

You can:

* Move across the country.
* Become a vegan.
* Leave a relationship that's making you unhappy.
* Accept your dream job even if it's for less pay.
* Make mistakes.
* Live an incredible story.
* Do anything you want (as long as it's not illegal. This book will not hold up as evidence in a court of law).

I didn't need permission to leave a job that disrupted my sleep, nor do you. Don't waste your time waiting on someone else to give you permission. Instead, be confident in your ability to make your own decisions, take risks and know your permission has already been granted.

Quitting isn't always a bad thing. Stop feeling so guilty about it already.

Write Your Quit List

EXERCISE

Working up the courage to quit things can sometimes feel like a challenge. We attach meaning to the things that were once important to us and often mourn the loss once we decide to quit them. Quitting isn't always bad; it can be a good thing. Make a list of things you have quit to remind yourself that sometimes quitting is necessary.

Trust The Timing Of Your Life

I don't know about you, but it seems like someone is always trying to rush the timeline of my life. My sister is always in my ear, telling me she doesn't understand why I'm not more famous online. (Sidenote: My sister is my #1 fan. I don't believe she's being malicious. She's just ready to see me on a billboard somewhere.) I've had coaches and mentors wonder aloud, "Why hasn't your business blown up yet?" I've had friends helpfully declare that I'm witty and charming enough that they know I'm the one who's going to "make it."

Occasionally, it stings to hear those types of comments. As if I don't want things in my life to happen faster or that I'm willing their vision of my success to take its sweet time to arrive. All those people fail to realize that my life, just like yours, has perfect timing. Everything happens in its own time and not one second before.

Case in point, I could only write this book at this moment in time and space. No other timing would have worked. Another time wouldn't have produced the book you're holding right now. I can say this because I've sat with the title and idea for this book for over three years. It started in the Summer of 2018, over a three-day ADHD-fueled period of hyperfocus where I couldn't stop thinking about how my fear voice sounded like a chorus.

By the end of that third day, I had written and designed a tiny book called *The Fear Guide*. Within a week, I convinced my friend Meg to let me present a talk on fear based on what I wrote in *The Fear Guide*. A month later, I was standing in front of a group of women, encouraging them to try Beanboozled jelly beans and do their best to silence the Chorus of Fear.

Months later, I realized I had more to say about fear, and I already had the perfect book title, *Don't Let Fear Have All The*

Fun. I've been in contract with this book idea ever since. Only now have the stars aligned perfectly to allow it to happen. Everything I needed to write the best book I could at this time in my life found its way to me.

You have to learn to trust the timing of your life.

It is not always an easy or fun thing to do. There will be times when you'll look around and see the people standing at the starting line with you racing ahead. You'll get impatient waiting for your time on the podium. Setbacks will happen. You'll lag behind. Frustration will set in. You'll feel discouraged. Every so often, the tears will sting your eyes, and you'll wonder aloud, "When will it be my time?"

Rest assured that your life has perfect timing for everything that has happened and will happen in the future. You can't influence it. You can't change it. All you can do is live your life and grow through it. Keep showing up. Do the work even when it feels like it doesn't matter. Take tiny action daily. Don't allow fear to have all the fun. Not even for one second.

Some things, like this book, are not ready the first time you encounter them. They need more time. You need more experience. Once they are ready, it's your job to be bold and seize the opportunity. You will make it happen, but only when the timing is right. And you'll know it is because the stars will align in a way that they didn't before.

ADVICE #8

Key Takeaways

1. Experiencing a failure or setback is a normal part of your life's journey. Learn to treat failure as an event instead of an endpoint.

2. Despite what you've been taught, quitting isn't always bad. It's just as important to know when it's time to call it quits on an idea, goal, or situation.

3. Trust the timing of your life. Everything has perfect and proper timing.

176

CONCLUSION

All The Fun

"You can see the world as filled with danger, I suppose it is, but it's also filled with wonder. And you're cheating yourself out of the wonder that is always there. It's right there, but you have to get out into it. You have to open the door, step out into the sunshine, and then it's right there."

MANYA DOTSON

You've made it to the end. I feel it is fitting to end with a final story, but first, I must make a confession. Don't worry. It's a part of the story, but I'm nervous about sharing it.

You see. I've spent this entire book trying to convince you that you don't need to be fearless. That it's ok to be afraid. And I fear what I must confess will make me seem a hypocrite. I can already sense the dark clouds of judgment rolling in. Deep breath. Big sigh. Here's my confession:

I have the word "fearless" tattooed on my right shoulder.

Wait! Before you slam this book shut in disbelief, please allow me to explain.

Do you remember back to the beginning when I told you everything in my life changed on September 30, 2012? That day, my brother Maurice Malcolm Junior was fatally injured in a motorcycle accident.

The experience of losing Maurice with so much life ahead of him rocked me to my core. He was my first sibling. My first brother. The oldest son. The quiet funny one. And at the young age of 26, he was gone.

Maurice's passing wasn't my first experience with death. I had lost young and older people, but this time was different. Everything changed. I felt like the Earth quaked, and when it stopped, I was left sitting amongst a pile of rubble. Forcing me to confront my mortality in a way I was unprepared for.

In my wildest dreams, I always imagined I would live an incredible life full of travel, career success, and leaving my mark on the world. I was doing none of those things because I was too afraid. It made me question why I wasn't living as the person that I believed myself to be. Why was my fear of being judged stronger than my desire to live a vibrant, fulfilling, and fun life? I was tired of living a life where I only dared to dream but not do. Everything had changed, and I was afraid of remaining the same.

To call Maurice fearless would be an understatement. He had the word tattooed on his right shoulder. Months after his death, I honored his memory with the same fearless tattoo. I downloaded a picture of him from his Facebook account and walked into the nearest tattoo parlor. Secretly, I hoped that seeing this tattoo every morning in the mirror as I stood brushing my teeth would allow a little of Maurice's fearless nature to flow through me.

It has been almost ten years. I'm still not fearless.

Being fearless isn't a prerequisite for living a big, full, and extraordinary life. If you only remember one lesson from this book, let it be this:

You don't need to be fearless to make bold moves in your life. You just need to summon the tiniest amount of courage necessary to take the next small step.

Scratch that. You've read this far. I want you to remember the most important pieces of wisdom I have shared.

- The Chorus of Fear is ready and waiting to sing you out of taking any risks. Don't let it. Your life will expand or contract to fit the spaces not occupied by fear.
- Get comfortable with being uncomfortable. Your need for comfort is silently killing your dreams, and you're paying the price with tolls on your life.
- When you become aware of your fear, acknowledge it, and name it, you take back your power.
- Stop romanticizing the worst-case scenario. Give more energy to thinking about the best that can happen. What if it worked out? How good could it get?
- You don't need to feel brave to get started. Courage isn't finite. The more you use, the more you generate. You can build courage by taking tiny action.
- Celebrating your progress, no matter the size, influences continued action. Robbing us of the joy of celebration is the Chorus of Fear's greatest trick of all.
- You need people. Your journey through life will take you through many stages, and at each point, you need support.
- Don't confuse failure with a setback. The only actual failure is quitting instead of trying again with better data.

Maurice had an intense passion for motorcycles. He understood the risks, of course, but this was his passion, and it brought him incredible joy. Sometimes, while riding his motorcycle, he would experience one of those moments when everything in life is just exactly right. One of those moments when...the air is at the perfect temperature. The breeze blows past your face. The stars shine like gems in the sky. You feel so free and liberated. You lose track of time, and there is no past or future, only the intense joy of the present moment. A state of absolute bliss.

These are the moments in life when you feel fully alive. We all have different things that bring this kind of bliss. For my brother, it was riding motorcycles. For me, it is spending time with people I love and enjoying deep belly laughs. For you, it might be singing, painting, dancing, writing, designing, sailing, hiking, the joy of developing a product, or building a business.

I've realized that you can't experience a moment like this if you are too afraid to make a move, too afraid even to try. You have to be afraid and do the thing anyway to get the reward.

You don't have to be 'fearless,' but you've got to be willing to take risks and do the thing that makes you feel bliss. We all have different levels of risk tolerance. You may not be willing to risk your physical safety or your life savings. You may not be willing to 'risk it all,' and that's okay. But, you have to risk 'something' to feel the reward. You have to be just the tiniest bit 'unsafe'. Playing it safe creates a very suffocating, small life with many regrets.

My brother left this earth sooner than anybody wanted, but I know he lived with no regrets. He did not allow fear to have all the fun. And that is why this book is dedicated to him.

No one is going to show up and hand you an extraordinary life. That's your quest. It's what you're here on this planet to discover, and you need to be willing to see it through like Frodo Baggins. So the challenge becomes not figuring out what you want but being honest with yourself about which of those dreams, goals, or secret desires you're ready to free from that big black garbage bag you've kept them tied up in.

What do you want so badly that it would be worth putting your ego on the line to get it? What would you be willing to wager or risk? What moves would you be willing to make? Would you be brave enough to tell the Chorus of Fear, "Be quiet. I got this," and take the next step?

I believe you're finally ready to answer those questions. Now, it's time for you to go and have all the fun.

SCIENCE
YES!

Resources

CELEBRATION PLAYLIST

* moniquemalcolm.com/celebration-playlist

WAYS TO CONNECT WITH ME

* Taketinyaction.com
* Moniquemalcolm.com/newsletter
* Youtube.com/c/moniquemalcolm

HELPFUL ARTICLES ABOUT PLANNING

* How to plan your week - https://moniquemalcolm.com/how-to-plan-your-week/
* How to plan your goals - https://moniquemalcolm.com/plan-your-goals/
* How to set S.M.A.R.T. goals the right way https://moniquemalcolm.com/how-to-set-smart-goals-the-right-way/

Sources of inspiration

PODCASTS

* Creative Pep Talk Podcast
  https://www.creativepeptalk.com
* 100 Tiny Actions Podcast
  https://www.100tinyactions.com

BOOKS

* *Untamed* by Glennon Doyle
* *Playing Big* by Tara Mohr
* *The Alchemist* by Paulo Coelho
* *Firekeeper's Daughter* by Angeline Boulley
* *The Night Circus* by Erin Morgenstern

Acknowledgements

Allow me to reintroduce myself because your girl is officially an author. I did it!

When I go on to glory, please don't forget to mention in my obituary that I was an author no less than three times. This is important! I spent a year working on this book and don't want anyone to forget. I will haunt you.

Jokes and threats to haunt my family aside, throughout the writing journey for this book, I described the process as an "endless rollercoaster of confidence and self-doubt." No one knows this better than the crew of people I leaned on throughout the creation of this book. This is your victory just as much as it is mine. We did it!

Please accept my heartfelt thanks in no particular order. (Seriously, I know how some of you are. Do not read anything into this order. If you come at me about why you aren't listed higher up, I will karate chop you.)

Writing a book costs money. Like a good amount of it. Many thanks to my love, Darrington for holding it down financially while I tried to write enough words to fill these pages. I'm stubborn. I really believed that I would be able to carry my normal workload while writing. You were right when you repeatedly told me to "just focus on writing your book."

Grandma Coffee, I hope your bags are still packed and ready. I don't know where this book will take me but you need to be ready to go at a moment's notice. Thank you for the prayers and continued encouragement.

Mommy, Daddy, Myria, and Chris—Thank you for being so

enthusiastic about my writing journey. Thanks for constantly checking in about my progress.

Khalil, you are my favorite little Krabby Patty.

A big shout out to everyone I interviewed for this book: Amber Wright, Elizabeth Fening, Amanda Shell, Alisha Robinson, Kenesha Osbourne, Taryn Jerez, Christa David, Alex "Nemo" Hanse, Manya Dotson, XayLi Barclay, Vic Benoit, Tami Hackbarth, Melissa Allen, Tyler Young, Andria Giles, and Christopher Malcolm. Thank you for sharing your story. I drew inspiration from your stories. Thank you for your vulnerability. Thank you for helping to make my book better.

There are too many friends to name. If you offered a kind word or showed enthusiasm for this book I appreciated it more than you know.

An extra big thanks to the entire Get It Done team! Your guidance during every phase of this book helped push me over the finish line. Thanks for seeing my vision, Alex and Lindsey.

Author Bio

Monique Malcolm is a multi-passionate creator. She's the founder of Take Tiny Action, a company that produces beautiful goal setting planners, stickers, and accessories, and the host of *100 Tiny Actions,* which is a podcast that offers tips for living a vibrant and fulfilling life. A frequent speaker at conferences and other events, Monique loves to speak onstage and motivate audiences to *"not let fear have all the fun."*

She lives in Florida with her husband and son. When she's not working, she loves soaking up the sun at the beach or hopping onto her bike for a spin class.

Learn more at moniquemalcolm.com and taketinyaction.com